Agile Reflections

*Musings Toward Becoming
"Seriously Agile"
in Software Development*

Robert Galen

Many of the designations used by manufacturers and sellers to distinguish their products are claimed as trademarks. Where those designations appear in this book, and the publisher was aware of the trademark claim, the designations have been printed with initial capital letters or all capitals.

The author and publisher have taken care in the preparation of this book, but make no expressed or implied warranty of any kind and assume no responsibility for errors of omission. No liability is assumed for incidental or consequential damages in connection with or arising out of the use of the information contained herein.

Cover Photo: *Dawn over Lough Leane, Killarney, with reflections in the water*. Photographer – Karl Jordan, stock photo from 123RF (www.123rf.com) , stock #6682207, licensed in Fall of 2012.

ISBN: 978-0-9885026-0-4

Printed in the United States

Appreciations

I first must thank the folks at <u>PM Times</u> and <u>BA Times</u> for supporting my blogging. In the beginning Ollan Delaney was the editor and he was an incredible pleasure to work with. He was the consummate editor, light in touch, while providing just the right amount of meaningful support, guidance and creative perspective. Unfortunately, <u>Ollan passed away</u> in November 2010. I miss him still.

Replacing Ollan was no easy task, but Cheryl Ricker has done an admirable job of editing and managing site content. She truly cares about the two sites and their readers. Cheryl is also tolerant of my occasional tardiness and tendency to over-deliver content. I'm incredibly thankful for Ollan, Cheryl, and all of the behind-the-scenes staff at DBC that have supported my writing.

The next group to truly thank is my "inspiration". By that I mean—where do the ideas come from? In my case, they come from my coaching, whether it's teams that I'm directly a part of or external coaching clients. My inspiration comes from the real world, including frustrations, challenges, patterns, and anti-patterns. From observations of behaviors that are limiting the capability of agile making a true impact within organizations, across teams, or with individuals.

My inspiration directly came from:

- My 2 ½ years at iContact
- Numerous coaching clients
- Discussions during my Meta-casts with Josh Anderson
- Interactions at conferences and training workshops
- Some work history with Teradata and ChannelAdvisor
- Our local Raleigh/Durham agile community
- And finally a short, but rich, stint at Deutsche Bank

I want to thank everyone that I've worked with on agile adoption. No matter how well or how poorly you've done, I honor your efforts, intentions, and everything I've learned from you. You've helped me to continually improve my agile coaching and servant leadership.

Specifically, I want to thank my ex-colleagues from iContact. Jeff Sutherland has talked for years about hyper-productive agile teams. It's never been clear to me what magic dust makes regular, high, or hyper performing agile teams. Is there a secret metric or a specific percentage increase in productivity? I honestly don't think so.

However, I do think agile done well has a particular 'feel' to it—in teams that are approaching "being Agile" in their mindset, daily activities, culture, and importantly, their results.

For 2 ½ years I was fortunate and lucky enough to help build and coach just such a set of teams at iContact. In many ways, I wouldn't be the coach I am today without the opportunity to partner with this group. It was a distinct privilege to work with such fine agilists. From where I sit, we were very much…hyper-performing!

In particular at iContact I want to thank Ralph Kasuba for giving me the chance to lead such a great team. Ralph is one of my role models for servant leadership done well and I greatly appreciated his trust and empowerment.

So, at the risk of leaving someone off the list, I want to thank these iContact folks for helping frame my ideas, my coaching focus points, my frustrations and challenges, and ultimately…my blog posts.

Thanks to: Autobots, Bill Bates, Geoff Catlin, Maureen Green, Tim Kykendall, Anne Moore, Jackie Owino, Andrew Parker, David Rasch, Mark Riedeman, Brian Sobus, and Mary Thorn.

Also thanks to our U/X team and our Product Team led by Michelle Engle. Our wonderful Product Owners included: Michelle, Peter Ghali, Rob Call, Alan Cox, Matt Davis, Eddie Howard, Jeff Ravetto, and Jeff Wright.

Next I need to give a special thank you to Josh Anderson. Josh and I have been Meta-Casting for close to rwo years. We are separated widely by age and experience, but I think we're very like-minded in our views towards agility. Josh certainly keeps me on my toes and honest about my evolving ideas surrounding "agility done well". Check out our Meta-cast podcasts here: www.meta-cast.com , while I'm clearly biased, I think they nicely compliment the book.

I want to again thank my family. My children have always been incredibly supportive of what I do. And my wife Diane has been a constant and tireless supporter. Diane, your patience and support now and always mean the world to me. Thank you for supporting what I love to do.

For those who know me, you know that Diane and I are fairly rabid pet lovers. During the time I was writing these blog entries, we lost our beloved dog Foster. We love ALL of our animals dearly. But Foster was special to us. He was more human than dog and we treasured the time we had with him.

I'm quite positive he had a strong influence (and still does) on my agile coaching. We miss you Fost-man!

And last but not least, I want to thank <u>you</u> for picking up this book, your interest in my thoughts, and for taking time out of your busy day. I hope you find something of value within…to help you in your own journey.

Stay agile my friends…

Contents

References for Pictures

1. Chapter 1 – Close up shot of red admit one tickets shot on white with soft drop shadow, BigStock Photo – stock #17109698
2. Chapter 2 –   Downloaded from internet @ http://airforcebasictraining.blogspot.ca/
3. Chapter 3 – Pile of old books with reading glasses on desk, BigStock Photo – stock #14091164
4. Chapter 4 – Nature jewelry store clerk assisting couple in choosing an engagement ring, BigStock Photo – stock #35573036
5. Chapter 5 – Helping Hands, BigStock Photo – stock #1698219
6. Chapter 6 – Peking Triad, BigStock Photo – stock #1175136
7. Chapter 7 – Fishing from a canoe on a misty morning, BigStock Photo – stock #20860310
8. Chapter 8 – Magic equipment, BigStock Photo – stock #7439765
9. Chapter 9 – Downloaded from the internet @
   http://pearleandpiercehome.com/tag/1987/ ,
   http://allenketchersid.com/2011/09/19/wheres-the-beef/
10. Chapter 10 – Rocks in night sea, BigStock Photo – stock #6636809
11. Chapter 11 – Nine skydivers in free fall, BigStock Photo – stock #10023701
12. Chapter 12 – One cat grooming another cat isolated on a gray background. BigStock Photo – stock #36771109, and Photo of bloodhound puppy dog. BigStock Photo – stock #32632577
13. Chapter 13 – Trust Concept, BigStock Photo – stock #34774721
14. Chapter 14 – Success, failure road sign, BigStock Photo – stock #1967195
15. Chapter 15 – Business team putting their hands, BigStock Photo – stock #24939839
16. Chapter 16 – Downloaded from the internet @
   http://www.intomobile.com/2010/09/23/sprint-cancel-early-termination-fee/
17. Chapter 17 – Regular or decaf coffee, BigStock Photo – stock #6857935
18. Chapter 18 – Drawing of a cars dashboard. BigStock Photo – stock #1092064
19. Chapter 19 – New York – November 25: The Spiderman float appears in the 84th Macy's Thanksgiving Day Parade on November 25, 2010 in New York City, BigStock Photo – stock #20138351 and Pig Picture was downloaded from the internet @
   http://allanimallife.blogspot.com/2009/08/bay-of-pigs.html
20. Chapter 20 – Canned organic tomato red sauce, 3 big jars, BigStock Photo – stock #23073728

Introduction

In July 2009, I started writing blog posts for BA Times and PM Times. Both portals are homed as part of Diversified Business Communications, a Toronto based media and training firm focused respectively towards the Business Analyst and Project Management communities. I'd been writing articles for some time and I've also written two books. But blogging was new for me and it was a challenge to find my voice and my style.

I also found that I had much more to say on the Project Management side of things. An example of that is a series I began called *The Agile Project Manager*. My intent in developing the series was to provide assistance to traditional project managers in evolving towards more agile practices and an agile mindset. In my mind, I counted them in the same group as front-line functional managers, who had to essentially transform in order to effectively operate within agile contexts.

On the business analysis side of things, I was simply trying to help BA's find their niche in agile. I liken BA's to be much like testers who also struggle to find their place; I wanted to provide some guidance as to what they could and should DO within agile teams.

So fast-forward a few years and I've written a lot of content—stories, advice, patterns, and of course anti-patterns across the blogs. Then something struck me. I realized that I might have enough relevant content to fill a book of shared lessons. There were a few holes in coverage that I filled by combining and editing some posts, but in general I felt there was a coherent set of lessons that might prove helpful in a single, consolidated place.

So that is the genesis in the thinking behind this book. In general, I'm looking to help improve agile teams by sharing my experiences. Certainly not in a prescriptive, I know it all way. But in a pragmatic way, so you can avoid my mistakes while accelerating your adoption.

I'm a Wordy Blogger

Most blogs I read are single-topic focused, quite modest and succinct. I'm actually amazed by those people and how they convey so much information in so few words. My original word count target for blogging was somewhere between 800-1200 words. I typically kept to these boundaries on the BA Times side of things. But I quickly started exceeding even these healthy limits with my PM Times posts.

Essentially, I started writing what were more articles, essays, or chapters for a book; rather than what would be considered condensed, blog snippets. The good news was that folks still seemed to be reading them. The bad news is that I strongly suspect the length did put quite a few off—so my messages weren't getting as broad exposure as I'd hoped.

Time...

As time moved on, I began to realize that the content I was producing for the blogs could be easily packaged into a book. That would have several advantages:

- The themes across different blog posts were lost in the blog; so any common threads or relationships were probably lost across the disparate posts. In a book, I could "connect the dots" better from post to post and even structure related posts together.
- Often you're in a hurry when writing for a blog and editing is a second-class consideration. I often made grammatical mistakes in blog posts. It was actually quite surprising that folks rarely brought these to my attention in comments. They were being extremely kind. Here I get another chance to clean things up a bit.
- Time was the enemy for the blog. Most of the readers surfaced in the first 2-3 weeks. If you didn't get to a blog post early, it would sort of lose its visibility as it "scrolled down" the blog backlog. Of if a post happened to hit a particular holiday or vacation period, the readership would inevitably be down. A book gives each post or chapter equal billing.
- Finally, a book allows me to "glue" content together, update content based on new learning, and complete some lessons that were a bit too short or too fragmented because of the blog format constraints.

How to Read the Book?

One of the advantages of basing the book on blog posts or articles is that each is relatively self-contained. Given that, I think you can start at any chapter in the book and get value from that individual discussion.

Sure, some of them are connected in some way and the individual sections are certainly within a theme. But feel free to pick it up, peruse the table of contents, and go where your heart or your challenges take you.

Sections

There are five focused sections to the book:

1. **Beginnings**— the art of the start; how to effectively begin your agile teams and projects
2. **Execution**— where the rubber meets the road I suppose…guidance around effectively iterating
3. **Customer**— the why and what behind agile teams; who drives the value and who you deliver to
4. **Mindset**— you can easily 'say' you're agile, but are you really?
5. **Leadership**— yes, we need 'stinkin' leadership. I think more so in agile teams than many believe

With all of that being said, I hope you find some value in the pages (physical or virtual) of this book and it helps you in your journey towards becoming *Seriously Agile*.

Enjoy and stay agile my friends,
Bob Galen

November 2012
Cary, NC

Section 1 – Beginnings

The first section of the book concentrates on starting agile well. I always loved the Stephen Covey point of "Beginning with the End in Mind" from his 7 Habits book. I think agile adoption and projects benefit from a focus and intentionality around starting well. Getting a sense for the landscape and doing a bit of planning before you "dive in" and start sprinting.

1. **Going Agile—The Price of Admission**
   - Many organizations want to take the least path of resistance towards agile adoption, but that might not be the best way.
   - http://www.projecttimes.com/robert-galen/the-agile-project-manager-going-agile-the-price-of-admission.html

2. **Agile Basic Training—What is an Acceptable Level?**
   - Thoughts around training, agile certifications and what is a sufficient level of training and practices to start your agile projects.
   - http://www.rgalen.com/blog/2012/6/25/the-agile-project-manager-agile-basic-trainingwhat-is-an-acc.html

3. **Agile Chartering—Critical to a Proper Beginning**
   - Setting up an agile project for success does need to happen. In fact, that traditional notion of a "Project Charter" works nicely for agile too.

4. **Engaging your Customer**
   - A critical success factor for any of the agile methods is continuous engagement by your customer or stakeholders.
   - http://www.projecttimes.com/robert-galen/agile-project-managementengaging-your-customer.html

Enjoy!

1—"Going Agile": The Price Of Admission

I often get asked to visit agile teams and deliver some ad-hoc training and coaching. As part of the coaching, I'm usually asked to do an informal assessment and share improvement feedback—framing the visit as part "getting to know each other" session and part agile assessment. A short while ago, I visited a team who had been doing agile (mostly Scrum) for quite a while, and considered themselves relatively mature in their adoption.

Almost immediately, as I got off the elevator, I noticed that their environment was open and airy, which is very conducive to collaborative agile teams. There were rolling whiteboards all around the office and small groups of people were pairing and collaborating everywhere. Even the managers were sitting out in open space.

So my anticipation grew as we walked around. I was looking forward to seeing some high-performance and mature agile team activities, as well as the subsequent results that such teams can deliver. There's nothing in the world quite as exciting as a well-honed agile team.

(I know, I know that's a geeky, agile coaching perspective…but they do excite me ;-)

The other exciting part of this organization is that they had invested in hiring some internal agile coaches. Again, that was a maturity indicator from my perspective, as they had experienced 'guides' for their agile journey; so call them Agile Coaches or Agile Project Managers.

The Teams

But as I physically sat down with the teams and interacted with them, I realized quite quickly that something was wrong. Drastically wrong. The teams seemed to be aimlessly "doing Agile". There was no sense of velocity, no sense of reliable burndowns, no sense of release planning, and each had no clear sense of commitment to where they were going. In a nutshell, the teams were in open space, there was an agile façade of sorts and they even had experienced coaches; but when you looked under the covers, there was no "consistency or directional substance". Here's an example of what I mean.

Backlog Grooming...Run Amok

One of the first meetings I attended was a *backlog grooming* session. I was introduced to 'John' as the Product Owner. He was going over some user stories with his team and they were estimating them. John went to the whiteboard and started writing down numbers. I was curious as to what he was doing. Then, he started to point to individuals and tell them what their estimates were for each individual story. He articulated architecture and design approaches, as he saw them, and basically shared with his "self-directed" team that he'd sorted out all of the "hard stuff" for them.

He seemed quite proud of the leadership he was providing. Their agile coach was also their Scrum Master. John was the functional manager for the team, as well as, their Product Owner. He also seemed to have assumed the role of Chief Architect and general oracle for the team. Clearly, there was lot of "role overloading" going on within this team.

At this point, I realized that I vastly underestimated the maturity of the teams. I had formed a perception from the coaches I'd met with and from the physical environment, but when you scratched the surface, the environment was culturally command-and-control oriented. They'd also seemed to be struggling with the people and focus investment that agile requires.

As I walked around the organization and became immersed in different teams, different projects, different instances of Scrum, etc., I realized that everyone was saying they were 'doing' Scrum and 'doing' Agile, but there was no rhyme nor reason to it.

There was also no consistency or standards in the practices. One team would be using user stories, but without any notion of, or investment in, acceptance tests. Another team would be spending nearly 90% of their development time ruthlessly designing cucumber tests, but their stories were poorly written and defined.

In some teams, a team member was encouraged (forced) to be a developer, as well as, the Scrum Master or Product Owner, without any proper training whatsoever. In other cases, functional managers were taking on Scrum Master and Product Owner duties for teams that reported to them. In these cases, you could see the teams deferring to their managers in decision-making.

There was literally, self-directed agile chaos. The only thing that was consistent across the various development groups was:

1. The had daily stand-ups
2. They had a sprint duration/tempo defined
3. They had whiteboards and used lots of cards
4. They had user stories and tasks for their current sprint
5. They tried to support the Scrum ceremonies of sprint planning, demo, and retrospective

As I sat down with their coaches and (gently) confronted them regarding this, they reacted poorly. Their overall reaction was that they were doing the "best they could" and stated that because the organization lacked the maturity and readiness for more mature agile practices adoption, they were introducing small changes in an effort to help where they could.

I felt quite sad afterwards.

I realize the coaches were trying to do the best they could and so were the teams. However, from my perspective, they were just "scratching the surface" of agile and not realizing much (if any) of the promise and benefit of "being Agile". It also made me wonder whether the coaches were actually doing their teams a service by only introducing them to the easier bits and pieces of agility and then allowing the over-customization of most of the core practices.

Another way of saying it—is it ok to only do 10% agile and leave it at that, even if the culture is challenging, or if the teams resist, or if the budget doesn't allow for it?"

Is that "good enough"?

The other key point is that by over-compromising, the coaches were not challenging the status quo within the organization. For example, all of the functional managers were strongly behaving in a command-and-control fashion. They should have received some training and coaching as part of the agile adoption—to, at least, introduce them to their need to and how to change their leadership behaviors.

ScrumBut

I don't think this organization is unique, nor do I believe I am the only one who's noticed "excessive compromise" in agile adoptions. Sometime around 2009, Ken Schwaber introduced the notion of a "Scrum-but", as in…"We're doing Scrum, but…" Here are some specific examples:

- We're doing Scrum, **but** we don't know our velocity
- We're doing Scrum, **but** our Manager is our Scrum Master and our Product Owner
- We're doing Scrum, **but** we're not a cross-functional team
- We're doing Scrum, **but** we've never really effectively planned and executed a sprint
- We're doing Scrum, **but** we don't really groom our Backlog
- We're doing Scrum, **but** we have 10 Product Owners directing our efforts
- We're doing Scrum, **but** we only have 10% of everyone's time to get our sprint work done

Apparently, he was noticing quite a bit of Scrum without the conviction associated with doing the majority of its practices well. What is frustrating is that every ScrumBut team likened themselves to "doing Scrum". From their perspective, they were actively leveraging it, but their implementations were mere shadows of the true intention of Scrum.

Now I do think Ken is a bit of a purist. His expectations seem to be that all teams should do 100% of Scrum, as he defines it in the Scrum Guide, in order to claim they are doing Scrum. I personally think that can be a bit harsh and unrealistic. However, I do feel there should be minimal levels of adopted practices that are required before a team claims to "be Agile" or "be using Scrum". That's where we're going next.

Should There Be a Price for Agile Admission?

The team I visited made me stop and think; I'm thankful to them for that. Think about whether it is ok to adopt miniscule and easier bits of the agile methods and still declare yourself to be agile. To fool yourself into thinking that you're already "good enough" and that whatever path you choose, all will equally drive the promises of agility—without the hard work.

I've always prided myself on being a pragmatist as an agile coach. I've certainly molded and crafted practices for teams that included compromises. I felt that agility meant that you were situational or context-based in your application of the various techniques and approaches.

And to a strong degree, I still feel that way. However, is there a point of diminishing returns? Where you compromise so much that the resulting practices are virtually worthless? And that the results you realize are so small or even negative in their impact? Or, actually do damage to the team and to the agile community?

I've come to the conclusion that the answer is "Yes"!

When we adopt agile, there should be an intentional price of admission. Call it a baseline of core agile practice support that you will achieve prior to going "Agile". For example, I don't believe you should be doing Scrum without a Scrum Master. Having a Scrum Master is a price of admission element to Scrum; here are some finer points around that notion:

1. Every Scrum team needs a dedicated or near-dedicated Scrum Master, someone with sufficient time to practice the craft of the role.
2. They should have a fundamental understanding of Scrum and have received some 'serious' training around the role and agile leadership. I'm not demanding a CSM certification, just some investment in solid external training.

3. It's incredibly bad form to have a manager assume the Scrum Master Role—particularly bad if their team also reports to them. Don't do that.
4. If they are multi-tasking between the Scrum Master role and another role (developer, tester, etc.) they shouldn't be the Scrum Master on a team where they're also an individual contributor.

If you can't support the above constraints in establishing Scrum Masters, then don't claim to be doing Scrum. This is simply one example of the entry criteria for Scrum. I went into more detail to make the point regarding one of the more important roles within a Scrum team.

Scrum Entry Criteria

Next I'd like to expand beyond the Scrum Master role and to look across the readiness criteria for a successful Scrum adoption. Here's what I would consider to be a proper short list of entry criteria, or the price of admission, for entering Scrum in your organization:

- You've introduced Scrum and Agile to your leadership team and they understand (and accept) the transitional role they need to play.
- You have a dedicated (focused) Scrum Master and dedicated (focused) Product Owner per team.
- You have formed dedicated (focused), cross-functional team(s).
- The teams have been trained in all aspects of Scrum and understand the various roles and their own responsibilities.
- You have a thoughtful Product Backlog per team, encompassing the project at-hand, which has been groomed by the team.
- The teams have completed release planning on their first project-level deliverable and have a sense for how to reach that goal.
- The Scrum Master(s) & Product Owner(s) have received separate training on the individual nuance of their roles.
- There are NO compromises with role overloading OR functional managers taking on roles across the team(s).
- The teams understand the notion of and expectations associated with operating as a self-directed team.
- The teams have an environment conducive to collaboration.

- The teams are committed to using low-fidelity tooling (cards, walls, whiteboards, team rooms, web cams, simple e-tools, etc.).
- Before starting their first sprint, the teams have a clear project mission, charter & goals that they can leverage in guiding and measuring their sprints.
- And finally at the risk of sounding self-serving, the teams have an experienced agile coach to rely on for guidance. (*somewhat optional*)

Too Prescriptive?

But, is it possible that the above list is too prescriptive?

I've often heard the argument for open-ended agility as being truly self-directed. The thought goes—how we can truly be agile and still hold prescriptive guidelines over a team?

My counterpoint to that is I'm mostly talking about Shu-level teams here and Shu-level organizations here (*interpret Shu as entry-level experience and there's a link for more research at the end of the article*). I believe a bit of prescriptive guidelines are necessary in order to set the stage for what "good Agile" looks like. It creates an environment for teams to mature so that they can effectively inspect and adapt their way towards higher maturity, performance and more self-directed practices.

I'm beginning to think that not setting clear entry criteria is a bit of an irresponsible copout. That, as coaches, we have gotten a bit lazy since it's much easier to coach agile teams without any entry criteria or guidelines, as you saw in my example. Shame on us!

Wrapping Up

This was a serious chapter topic focus for me in that it's challenged the very core of my flexibility and pragmatism in my own agile coaching. I think determining what to baseline, and how to approach agile adoption, is a deeply situational and personal choice for most Agile Project Managers and Coaches.

However, as a discipline we might be erring too much on the side of too little. Call it a lack of courage or willingness to take a stand. I don't try to understand all of the drivers. But, for my own coaching, I'm going to be asking more of my teams going forward in their initial agile practices. Not in the search for perfection, but in the search for a "meaningful set" of initial practices that are hard, drive improvement, and fosters an environment of "agile done well" throughout the teams.

Another way of saying it, I don't think we can truly call ourselves Agile Project Managers and coaches if we're fostering "10% Agile" as it simply doesn't provide the value or bang for the buck vs. the effort. And it also does the agile community a distinct disservice.

Thanks for listening,
Bob.

References & Follow-up

1. Online version of the ScrumBut test
2. A counterpoint to my "seemingly forceful" diatribe; Rachel makes the case for not being too forceful…
3. Shu-Ha-Ri to help with my Shu-level references

There's an interesting article or paper entitled Scrum "Shock Therapy" from Scott Downey on Jeff Sutherland's website. The link is here - http://scrum.jeffsutherland.com/2012/01/scrum-shock-therapy-how-to-change-teams.html
It's a nice compliment to this chapter in that it challenges the notion of balancing self-direction against firm leadership and prescriptive agile practices for new or forming teams. I'd recommend reading and considering the thoughts and implications.

2—Agile Basic Training: What Is An Acceptable Level?

The agile methods are deceptively simple and common sense oriented. In many ways, that's one of their great strengths, but is also one of their fundamental weaknesses. I see so many teams convinced that they can "go Agile" just by reading a book or an article and then diving in and 'sprinting' towards successful software delivery. The logic goes that agile is simple common sense practices, self-directed, and intuitive—so, of course, it will be simple to pick up and execute.

I typically categorize these teams as "bad Agile" teams. They adopt a small, superficial, and somewhat trivial, set of the core agile practices and then they believe they're practicing Agile. In almost every case, they don't understand the agile mindset or how the core principles and practices complement one another to foster improvement. They're "doing Agile", but they're not "being Agile".

As we explored in the last chapter, Ken Schwaber coined the term ScrumBut to capture this common anti-pattern. He was solely focused on Scrum in coining the term. However, I've found the extreme programming practices to be a complementary set of agile practices that are often left out of the conversation as well.

One of the core drivers for this is that teams don't receive sufficient agile training from the right level of experienced coaches and trainers. So, yes, you can pin some of the blame on the teams themselves. However, I think some of the assumptions we've set in the agile community are also to blame.

In this post, I want to explore what types of training are sufficient to get agile teams up and going. In this case, I'll be using Scrum as the baseline methodology for the discussion. But, you could essentially replace Scrum with Extreme Programming, Kanban, or any other agile methodology as I think the points generally remain the same.

Before we go after training in general, I want to explore certifications, many of which have a strong training component as part of their adoption.

Agile "Spaghetti" Certification Choices

There are essentially seven certifying bodies at the moment with respect to agile—sort of a spaghetti-like set of choices to make. In a nutshell, they include:

1. Scrum Alliance: the venerable institution that certifies Scrum Masters (CSM, CSP) Product Owners (CSPO), Coaches (CSC) and Certification Trainers (CST). There is some movement towards individual team member qualification as a Certified Developer (CSD), which focuses on hands-on development practices. When I sampled the website for this chapter, there were over 130,000 Certified Scrum Masters, over 130 Certified Scrum Trainers, and over 40 Certified Scrum Coaches. Clearly, the Scrum Alliance is still the leading certification body in this space.

2. Scrum.org: this is Ken Schwaber's group that is a historical spin-off from the Scrum Alliance. He started it after breaking with the Alliance Board. Aligned with the Scrum Guide, he's established a 2-tier certification for the Scrum Master and the Product Owner. Scrum.org also has a very strong offering targeted at the developer or practitioner. This is more or less a direct competitor to the Scrum Alliance (CSD) and may be a stronger offering than it is. Arguably, Scrum.org focuses more on assessments and practitioner-level skills. It's also clearly not as widely known as the Scrum Alliance, but it does seem to be gaining ground.

3. <u>Net Objectives</u>: have been focusing on more enterprise level and lean agile training for quite some time. They also offer certifications as part of their training offering, two examples being Agile Project Manager and Product Owner. It's more of a niche certification, although they're very well respected in the Lean, Kanban, and Enterprise Agile spaces.

4. <u>ICAgile</u>: is more of a generic Agile BOK (Body of Knowledge) certification authority. They provide sensible "outlines" for what good courseware should cover in specific areas of agile and they "certify" materials and provide certification management mechanisms. They don't provide a certification per se; they provide trainer material consistency and transparency assurances. A promising part of ICAgile is the breadth of their purview—virtually covering all areas of agile practices and not simply Scrum Master or Product Owner roles. Definitely a work-in-progress though.

5. <u>Dean Leffingwell - SAFe</u>: has begun to dominate the enterprise / scaling agile space and is offering a certification around his scaling framework. He calls it a Scaled Agile Framework (SAFe) and is offering *various levels* [1] of certification for its implementation. He is delivering the certification via his <u>Scaled Agile Academy</u>. To be fair, this is a brand new initiative and, even though Dean is well-respected, it's not clear we need this certification in the marketplace.

6. <u>CAT – Certified Agile Tester</u>: mostly a European-centric certification, this is the only tester focused certification out there. If you review the website, there aren't too many certified testers yet, perhaps +/- 200, so I'd consider this a beta and somewhat experimental at the moment. The primary customer seems to be European testers, probably because of the intense general certification interest there.

---

[1] As of this writing, there are apparently 4-levels of SAFe certification that Leffingwell and his team are offering. All directed towards larger-scale, agile Enterprise teams.

7. PMI-ACP: finally, the venerable Project Management Institute (PMI) has entered the fray with the Agile Certified Practitioner or PMI-ACP certification. After running a beta test in late 2011, there were over 2000 certified practitioners as I write this chapter in May 2012. Beyond the certification, there is a Community of Practice and the PMI seems to have embraced the notion of agile. The guidelines for certification are quite loose at the moment; being driven mostly by a "reading list". PMI has yet to develop an "Agile BOK – Body of Knowledge" upon which to more fairly base the certification.

8. IIBA: while not directly certifying BA's from an agile perspective, the IIBA has defined an Agile Extension to the BABOK Guide. It's a collaborative effort between the IIBA and the Agile Alliance to establish a baseline definition. Between ICAgile and IIBA, you probably get the best BOK-related references. However, it's currently unclear how they'll be leveraging it in their certification programs.

The fact that there are so many certifications and how quickly they've grown beyond the Scrum Alliance is a testament to the popularity and pervasiveness of the agile methods. Still, I can't help but think that the sheer number of options dilutes the value from a certification-holder perspective and from a prospective employer perspective. How in the world do you select a path through this mass of spaghetti?

The other problem is that the majority of them place a focus on prescriptive knowledge acquisition (reading and memorization), as well as, traditional testing. Very few of them emphasize real-world experience and verify that with more serious examination and proof. The Scrum Alliance CSC attempts to set a very high bar for entry and the numbers bear that out, while very few of the other certifications attempt to do that.

Most often the recipe is to study a set of materials, then take and pass a requisite test. At that point you will have the credential. In a methodology that places so much on inspect and adapt hands-on experience; this really doesn't pave the way for practical and situational experience.

For example, my personal preference is for Scrum Masters to acquire real-world experience, which trumps all of the certifications. I'd much rather hire a person who's been in an active Scrum Master role for 1-2 years than someone who's simply acquired a certification and assumes they can map their general experiences towards the role.

Body of Knowledge(s) and Consistency

The other thing that is somewhat lacking across the certifications is consistency.

For example, and to their credit, the PMI and the IIBA both have developed a Body of Knowledge, or BOK, that is the basis respectively for the PMP and CBAP credentials. The BOK clearly identifies the areas of study and competency that a holder of the credential must achieve in order to receive it.

While you may disagree with what's in the BOK, at least it provides a consistent baseline for the certification. I believe this is what ICAgile is trying to achieve by reviewing course materials across the various agile skill areas.

Most of the other certifications don't baseline themselves on a transparently established BOK so there is widely disparate coverage of the topic based on which instructor or trainer you choose. The CSM is notorious for this since each CST (Certified Scrum Trainer) has their own set of material and covers the topics that they believe most relevant for the certification.

While this is allows wonderful flexibility for the CST, attendees can get very different views. I know of one company that sent employees to two different CSM classes taught by two different trainers because of geographical distribution. When they pulled these folks together on teams, they found that they didn't have the same understanding of basic Scrum and agile practices. It caused the teams' tremendous start-up pain and needed additional coaching to get the teams on a level playing field from a core skills perspective.

That wouldn't have happened with improved consistency amongst CST's. Additionally, I don't think the burden of discovery should be solely on the client in these cases.

Even the PMI-ACP lacks a BOK. What they do recommend is a "reading list" of 10-12 agile books that serve as the core of the certification. That's an awful lot of reading and little real-world experience.

So be wary of how each certification quantifies its coverage and look for some semblance of consistency either by basic BOK definitions or by partnering with a specific coach or trainer to better understand their philosophies and content delivery.

Back to Basic Training

When I kick-off a Scrum team, I have four levels of basic training that I'm trying to instantiate within the organization, including:

1. **Team-level:** training the entire set of teams that will be initiating Scrum in the core methods. Usually this is a short class, 4-8 hours, with several workshops or games that illustrate the core behaviors of agile teams. This gets <u>everyone</u> on a level playing field for the method, roles, terminology, and basic practices.

2. **Product Owner-level:** training the selected Product Owners and the entire product organization in the nuance of User Stories, Product Backlogs, and Road-map Planning techniques. I'll usually coach them until they have a well-established backlog for their first release and have a solid tempo of grooming meetings established.

3. **Scrum Master-level:** this training can take the form of sending individuals to CSM (or similar) classes, or running an internal class that focuses on the role. I prefer the latter approach and then jump-starting the Scrum Master towards operating in their roles. After 3-6+ months if they want to go for a CSM, they can do it from a position of experience.

4. **Organizational Leadership-level:** training here focuses on the role shift for managers and executives in moving towards Scrum and agility. Addressing the requisite changes in their roles and how they have to adapt for effective agile adoption. I'll also review organizational transformation strategies for specific functions, for

example: the Project Management Office, or Testing Center of Excellence.

I think that a team shouldn't be "going Agile" without these four levels of basic training in place. They don't have to be exhaustive. In fact, all levels can be delivered in 2-3 days, but the overall balance in understanding they provide is often crucial for an organizations' adoption.

Beyond the training, I don't think you simply "walk away" and let these teams fend for themselves. As we'll explore next, coaching is also a very important part of agile adoption and a responsible thing to do.

Training without Coaching is Irresponsible

As I alluded to earlier, agile training and certifications are IMHO virtually useless without real experience and that experience isn't gained without coaching and mentoring.

I'll use a real story to make the point.

I was working with a team on starting up their adoption of agile. I came in and ran what I'd call an Agile / Scrum 101 session—equivalent to an abbreviated CSM class. Everyone on the projected teams attended the course as we setup the Scrum teams and product backlogs; preparing to start sprinting.

As a coach, I was given the opportunity to kick-off the first round of sprints. But, then something wonderful and also something terrible happened. The client felt confident with their skills; I guess I'd done too good a job of training. So soon after starting, they told me that they felt comfortable on their own and didn't need any additional coaching.

I tried to convince them that having a coach around in the beginning was a very, very good idea; but they felt they had it down and declined. Six to nine months elapsed and I checked in on them a few times via email. The VP of Development kept saying that things were going 'swimmingly' and they were truly enjoying agile development and the results.

Then somewhere around the nine month mark, I received a strange phone call. Things were "off the rails" and they wanted me to come in and assess what was happening. When I arrived, I quickly agreed with their assessment. You could barely tell that they were applying the principles which they had been taught and now there was tremendous distrust between the leadership and teams; driving a lack of transparency and truth-telling. I was not totally surprised, but I was incredibly disappointed that they hadn't called me sooner.

We quickly rectified the issues and they've since become a stable, mature, and continuously improving agile organization. They've also agreed that ongoing, periodic coaching is a necessary part of their agile adoption until they gain more experience, maturity, and sustainability.

That's one of the key points I wanted to make in this chapter. The agile methods are deceptively simple and often newbie teams want to go it alone with too little training and little to no initial coaching. In most-all cases I think they're making a HUGE mistake. Agility is very much of a mentored and experiential approach to software development.

You'll want to engage an experienced coach to help you adopt the basic tactics towards "doing Agile". But also to help you internalize the core behavior changes at all tiers in your organization towards "being Agile", so that you truly gain the benefits of adoption to drive business value across your organization.

Wrapping Up

Solid agile project managers can be a strong influencing point in early stage adoption. You can help the organization plan for training and ongoing coaching. You can encourage your teams to acknowledge their need for help and have the courage to ask for it as early as possible.

You'll realize that having experts around is not a sign of weakness, but truly a sign of strength.

Another area where you can help guide your organization is across the spaghetti confusion from all of the certification options. While training and certifications are an important part of adoption, you can provide the balance to help everyone understand that agile is about "the doing". So, having practical experience and gaining it with effective mentoring, is truly a crucial part of your maturation and growth.

Thanks for listening,
Bob.

3—Agile Chartering: Critical to a Proper Beginning

I was a new coach joining an agile team who had just started a new project. I joined after a few sprints, somewhat mid-stream, as they were sprinting to deliver their first release. It was a financial firm which was upgrading a very important application in their IT portfolio. It was an eight year old application that had simply been outgrown by the firm's fundamental and M&A driven growth.

It also did not support some of their new clients in Europe and the Far East; therefore, a cosmetic and fundamental upgrade that would handle transactions for about ten new countries was also needed. The team had committed to a 12-sprint release plan and, when I arrived, they were completing sprint 4—approximately one third of the way through the project.

When I joined the team, I felt rather good about the project. They were a dedicated and lively bunch of professionals who seemed on top of the project. From my perspective, they might have been a bit over-staffed for the effort, but I'd rather have too many people engaged than too few.

Expectations?

But quite soon I began hearing from their leadership team about their expectations for what would be delivered at the end of the release. As I started to attend daily stand-ups, review the team backlogs (there were actually four teams involved in the effort), and examined work burndown history and progress, I got a sinking feeling in the pit of my stomach.

The team was nowhere near being able to deliver on the expectations of the leadership team. Let me give you a sense of where things stood:

- The team was 33% of the way through the release plan, but only about 5-10% of the way through the work they had committed to from the stakeholders' perspective. They truly did not know exactly where they stood, because there was no clear understanding of the work. And as they continued to sprint this gap seemed to be widening, not closing.

- The team was still struggling with teamwork and collaboration. There was an important architectural team in China that was not very well integrated with the rest of the teams. They were working hard, but apparently on the wrong things—and delivering too slowly.

- I realized that the team did not have a release plan of any sort. Even their current backlog did not contain all of the work which they had committed to for this project. They were sprinting along, one sprint at a time, figuring things out as they went.

- There was a design element (UX) to the project. The interesting thing was that the design team was looking for a complete overhaul of the application, yet the level of effort and time allotted for the project clearly did not support this.

- Critical team members had been included in the budget and plans, but had not yet been hired. Indeed, there was some dragging of feet around fully staffing the teams. Consequently, the current commitment was based upon quite a few nonexistent team members.

What Happened?

The root of the teams problems truly centered on their leadership team. Leaders in this organization were accustomed to pulling together estimates and making project commitments for their teams. Typically, a set of managers and directors would get together and size up a project. They would then determine the feature set, complexity, and basic level of effort. They would also determine what team sizes and skills were required for that particular project. After that, they would look at ongoing work, assume end points, and fit new work in as they envisioned old work being completed.

In this case, since the team and approach were 'Agile', the leadership team had made the estimates in sprints. So, they had done the arithmetic and determined that it would take 4 teams 12 sprints to complete the work. They pulled together a PowerPoint deck that illustrated the plan and what the business would receive as a result of the release. Then they got approval for the project budget and assigned teams to begin the work.

Life was good!

But, from an Agile perspective, they had forgotten a few things. First, they forgot that this approach historically had not worked very well for them. They had an atrocious track record of project success, perhaps less than 10% approaching a successful conclusion. This was one of the very reasons that they chose to "go Agile". They hoped to improve upon this.

They also forgot that Agile was indeed, at its core, a team sport. That leadership needed to include the entire team in work planning as well as the work itself. That a team needed to commit to a body of work by getting familiar with the details and not some superficial estimate by people who would not ultimately be a part of the team nor contributing to the work.

Finally, they lost sight of the very essence of Agile leadership, which is to serve the team. They needed to set them up for success, while fostering an environment of self-direction and accountability, not set their teams up for failure, which they had clearly and firmly done.

Don't get me wrong. The leaders were not "bad" in this organization. Indeed, they were highly experienced, technically astute, and well intentioned. Their critical mistake was that they had moved their teams towards an Agile approach for software development, but forgot to shift their own project instantiation practices, behaviors, and patterns. It was a fundamental mistake that many organizations shifting towards agility make.

It Was a Train Wreck Waiting to Happen

With that entire context in place, the project was inevitably a train wreck in progress:

- The stakeholders were expecting something they would never receive in the allotted time and budget.
- The team was still forming and figuring out roles, responsibilities, work breakdowns, and who was best focused on what work.
- The UX team was trying to make this project their hallmark for usability and modern look and feel – over-designing everything.
- The development team had not even thought through the work, nor the estimated level of effort. They were just "winging it".
- And the cherry on top was…the clock was ticking!

This was a situation where business expectations were clearly misaligned with the team's capabilities. So, how do you realign something like this?

I'm glad you asked.

Agile Project Chartering

I realize it took me quite a long time to set the stage for this article. However, I think the context is useful. In a word, the organization failed to effectively <u>charter</u> their project. It's that simple. They did not connect the stakeholder needs, wants, desires, and expectations with the team's ability to deliver on those expectations. To me, that is the key driver of the chartering process—to set the stage for both "sides" of a project so that each understands the other and that there is alignment of effort towards a common and feasible goal.

Agile project chartering can contain many activities and can create specific artifacts. ALL are directed towards clarity in purpose in delivery. So, what are some of the activities surrounding Agile charters and the act of chartering itself?

The following come to mind:

- Establishing a vision and mission, while defining an overarching project goal.
- Clearly establishing what ultimate success "looks like".
- Establishing the team: structure, budget, equipment, tooling, recruiting and hiring, workspace, skill-sets, training, etc.
- Establishing the scope, including product backlog(s), minimal marketable features, and minimal marketable product definitions.
- Performing release planning: end-to-end, from concept to deployment; including customer usage planning.
- Establishing how success will be measured (usage, costs, revenue, what?)
- Performing risk planning to include clear communication, risks and mitigations, and actions.
- Establishing critical constraints – Doneness Criteria, Entry Criteria, and Release Success Criteria.
- Developing technical architecture and design; prototyping (planned research spikes) and establishing lab infrastructure.
- Communicating clearly what the team can (and cannot) deliver.
- Then, finally, achieving business and team commitment to the project and starting…

As you can see, these are all start-up related activities. I liken them to establishing a trip map or game plan for where you are going. They provide sufficient "directional clarity" so that everyone is on the same page and feels good about the feasibility and clarity of the project.

Sprinting to Hell…and Hopefully Back Again

I often see an anti-pattern in many Agile teams where they begin sprinting too soon. Why, perhaps because they can. Or perhaps because there is such a strong emphasis in most of the Agile methods on little to no upfront planning—towards simply diving in and sprinting.

The need to begin coding and iterating is often great in many Agile teams and cultures. That is perfectly fine IF you know where you are going and IF you are aligned with your project stakeholders. But, what if you are not? As in my example, the team was sprinting towards hell. They had no chance of meeting expectations, which is certainly NOT Agile.

If you are starting a new project, or find yourself misaligned with stakeholder and business expectations, I recommend pausing your sprints or iterations. Then nail down your critical unknowns and confusion factors. Next go through appropriate chartering steps to fill in the details. As a case study, let's see how the above team recovered from their challenging situation.

How Did the Team "Recover"?

It is often the case that I tell a story as a means of entering a discussion, but then I do not go back to revisit the example. I want to alter that pattern here. Let's go back and go through the steps that this team made to realign their project and themselves with a feasible and clear goal.

Admitting They Needed Help

The first thing that had to happen was the team (and their leadership team) admitting that something was wrong. From my perspective, it was clear. Whenever I compared the team's state with expectations, there was a clear gap. However, not everyone saw that gap. In fact, very few did.

There was an overriding sense that the team and their leadership wanted to keep sprinting, while telling their stakeholders that everything was fine. Both sides were virtually keeping their heads in the sand.

Breaking out of that cycle was the first step. The good news was that the gap was so large and so compelling that no one could really continue to ignore it. In general, it's usually quite difficult for teams to admit that they are in trouble and need help…even in Agile teams. Eventually everyone admitted that they were in trouble and needed help.

Then Pause…

At this point, they chose to pause and reflect. It is impossible to describe to you how hard this was for everyone. Remember, the clock was still ticking for the team and it seemed counterintuitive to stop and reassess the project (re-planning, if you will). Nonetheless, that was exactly what they needed to do.

The term Sprint #0 was used to label the event and it was mostly focused on a re-plan of the release by the team. The greatest focus for the team was on establishing three things:

1. A clear view of a Minimal Marketable Product definition that could be used to align with stakeholders.
2. A clear backlog that included all work for the project and connected back to the MMP.
3. A committed release plan that crossed all four teams and included dependencies, integration, and testing.

Obviously, there was resistance on the part of leadership to use any terminology that implied a 'pause', as it indicated that they had started the project prematurely and were now 'wasting' even more time. However, they ultimately agreed that it was the right language and the right move.

There was resistance within the team as well. The UX folks were happily designing 'ahead' for the project and did not want to stop. The developers were happily coding and did not want to stop either; working on what they perceived as 'documentation'. There was an overwhelming sense that activity and movement were better than alignment with a shared goal. This surprised me quite a bit.

Focus on Release Planning

The central activity surrounded what is normally called release planning. That involved writing and refining the set of stories related to the release. It also involved estimating them and 'fitting' sets of stories into sprints.

This was an incredibly iterative process. In many cases, about 20% of the time, the team would not have a clue about a story—even though it had been "in play" for their previous commitment. In those cases, we encouraged the team to do a bit of research or prototyping, so they could estimate the story and its relationships to help others work more effectively. Call it a "mini research spike" if you will.

Each day the team would spend about four hours as a group doing backlog grooming and release planning. The remaining time was spent with individuals and pairs working on their own. All work was aimed at obtaining a solid release plan and at the team understanding and being able to make a commitment to the release.

Ultimately, that was their exit criteria for the Sprint #0. The stakeholders supported the content which the team could commit to for a release that met the organizational and project goals.

Minimal Marketable Features / Product

During grooming it became clear that the team needed a quick, concise view as to what they were expected to release. It turned out that the product backlog was too detailed and contained too much information for everyone to understand the overall intent.

To help their understanding, we then asked the Product Owners to come up with a single sheet (PowerPoint slide) that represented the key requirements, or features, that were considered "<u>must haves</u>" for the release. This was called this a Minimal Marketable Product definition which contained a set of Minimal Marketable Features.

Once they did this, it actually helped the team "stay on point" in terms of what was in, or out, of play for the release. The MMP was then continuously referenced and modified as required. Another interesting thing happened. As I mentioned earlier, the UX team was very rambunctious in their design creativity and innovation. This was driving the overall time/cost of the project beyond realistic bounds. It was also frustrating the other teams, particularly the developers, because they were continuously defending the level of effort to actually implement the design ideas.

We finally asked the Product Owners and the UX team to pull together a MMF for the UX aspects of the project. In addition, we asked them to rationalize and vet this with the entire team as to whether it fitted into the project goals, vision and overall schedule targets. This worked extremely well in constraining the UX work to what truly could fit into the project's charter and allotted time.

Moving the Line...Towards Commitment

Because the release plan cut across four teams, we could not commit to it unless <u>all</u> the teams had their work (and dependencies) identified and reconciled in the release plan. We took an approach of working left to right on a swim lane-based board for each of the sprints. We moved an indicator as we achieved commitments across all four teams for each sprint's work—leading towards our ultimate number of sprints to deliver on the MMP goal.

This visual method of indicating each sprint as we gained x-team buy-in to the work proved to be a wonderful device for all of the teams. Also, it was not unheard of for the indicator to move _backwards_ as we uncovered an unplanned dependency that needed to move back and then reconcile forward.

Negotiation and More Release Scenario Planning

The first time we approached the business stakeholders with our initial release plan, they were shocked. They had assumed that the team could do so much more than what the planning now illustrated was possible. Given this difference, there was quite a lot of emotionally charged discussion.

First, they threatened to cancel the project because it did not deliver sufficient value given the time and budget. That attitude passed quickly. Then the "AHA" moment occurred when they realized that, although they might not be getting everything they wanted, the team had a thoughtful, well integrated release plan and a solid understanding of the work.

Next, they sent back for a variety of scenario changes. They wanted the teams to look into options for variations to the project scope. The good news was that, by now, the team was quite adept at cross-team scenario planning and, in another week, presented back the scope versus time trade-offs for each variation. More importantly, the team and the Product Owners made some firm recommendations as to which direction they felt was best—not only from a business perspective, but also from a product technology perspective.

Finally...Commitment!

This section is short. The business stakeholders finally selected a scenario and the team committed to that release plan. Then the sprinting began again. However, this time they were ALIGNED with the business AND they had a baseline release plan against which to map any changes as they made further discoveries.

Arguably, they should never have started the work without this in the first place. But they did get there eventually.

An Important Key to Success

There is one final point to this scenario that I want to make. The Product Owners were <u>central</u> to the team's success during this realignment. Not only did they have to work with the team on story writing and developing MMP views, but they had to defend the team from external misperceptions. In a word, they were the bridge between the realities emerging from the team's planning activities and the needs of the stakeholders. We were lucky that we had two well respected, hardworking and very agile Product Owners representing the teams.

Wrapping Up

This post reflects why I think traditional project managers have a place within agile teams. Those project managers know how important chartering is, how important alignment is, how important it is to clearly communicate and manage expectations, and how important it is to get off to a good start.

Nowadays, agile teams do not need traditional chartering activities. The terminology and focus needs to be quite different. However, the essence of the activity is the same and many more Agile teams need to charter than think they do.

The example I presented, at least in my mind, is all about Agile chartering. I hope you can see that and hope you take away some lessons on what <u>not</u> to do and what <u>to do</u> when you are beginning agile projects. Agile project managers should be very good at guiding and leading just-in-time chartering activities within their teams. Do not <u>ever</u> lose sight of what Stephen Covey calls "Beginning with the End in Mind"!

Thanks for listening,
Bob.

References

1. I did not mention it in the article, but there is a wonderful book that focuses on chartering under the title <u>Liftoff: Launching Agile Teams and Projects</u> by Diana Larsen and Ainsley Nies. It generally covers the basics of chartering with a heavy agile context. Highly recommended!
2. Basic information - <u>http://www.projecttimes.com/articles/meet-your-new-best-friend-the-project-charter.html</u>
3. Basic information - <u>http://www.agilesherpa.org/agile_coach/product_planning/chartering/</u>
4. InfoQ article on some basic aspects of establishing an agile charter - <u>http://www.infoq.com/news/2010/05/agile-project-charter</u>
5. This is referenced in the InfoQ article - <u>http://michaellant.com/2010/05/18/how-to-make-your-project-not-suck/</u>
6. Here is a wonderful look at ten steps for project inception - <u>http://agilewarrior.wordpress.com/2010/11/06/the-agile-inception-deck/</u>
7. This is more of a traditional PM to Agile PM checklist-oriented mapping. Something I might not recommend doing, but a good example of something you might, nonetheless, need to try in certain contexts - <u>http://www.projectsatwork.com/content/articles/272704.cfm</u>

4—Engaging Your Customer!

The agile methods come at software development by challenging many of our status quo practices. The first one is the engagement level of the 'customer'. It's my experience that most waterfall or traditional projects allow the customer to disengage after they start the project and provide an initial version of the requirements. After some time, usually at the end of the project, they reappear to receive their 'prize'. Frequently, they're disappointed in the end result, quickly finding the functionality not living up to their original vision and expectations.

This sort of "end-points" behavior leads to many project failures due to a lack of clear communication, which leads to misunderstanding and missed expectations.

However, it has a simple solution. The customer should stay engaged during the entire project. They should be available for trade-off discussions and for demonstrations. They should provide ongoing feedback on interim deliverables. They should even understand the teams' capabilities and implementation challenges. In a word, they should become a '<u>partner</u>' to the team and not simply a '<u>stakeholder</u>'. They need to have continuous skin in the game if the project stumbles, as they need to be a part of trade-off and scope adjustment decisions.

The agile methods have several ceremonies or tactics that are intended to draw the customer towards the team; to foster their inclusion and to gain their insights. In this chapter I want to review and emphasize the importance of these practices and the overall need for customer engagement.

Backlog Grooming

You all know that a prioritized backlog of work items (prioritized features, large, tasks, key functional and non-functional requirements) is what drives the agile 'machine'. The list is dynamic in nature with items being added, removed and changed nearly continuously during the lifetime of an agile project.

Many agile authors and coaches represent the central nature of the backlog as a pyramid or iceberg. It follows then that at the 'tip' is where the highest priority items are found. They are also defined at the clearest and finest level of granularity. In other words, these items are 'ready' for execution. The team has sized them and broken them down. They have discussed and explored them several times as they've done this.

This activity is typically called 'grooming' the backlog. It's where the team repeatedly revisits the backlog, refining it from multiple perspectives and getting elements ready for execution. The Scrum product backlog is not only a list of features, but it's effectively a work breakdown structure for all of the work necessary to complete a product or project release.

By involving your customers and stakeholders in backlog grooming and making it transparent, you're engaging them at a base level of requirement management and project planning. Both are areas where your transparency can and should pay-off in increased interaction and pre-execution feedback on the backlog.

It also results in a better understanding on the part of the stakeholders for the level of complexity and difficulty that the team is encountering. I probably hear pushback 3-5 times in every grooming session around how easy attending stakeholders thought a feature would be to complete. Why, we almost do it now, so it can't take more than an hour or so to extend the feature…right?

Then the team patiently tries to explain why the design is more complex and how the estimate for the story is extended by the "real world" they deal with every day. Or why a single day implementation might need three days of testing because of data security concerns. Having the customer involved in grooming and planning can help them understand why things take as long as they do, while also drawing them into powerful trade-off discussions.

Sprint Planning

Rarely does an approach to software development include customers and stakeholders in planning the project. At least not in the nitty-gritty details of the effort. But in Scrums' sprint planning ceremony the customer is welcome to attend as the team considers the work and plans their execution.

The meeting has a two-phased approach. Phase one is focused towards the Product Owner sharing the sprints' focus with the team. They review the body of stories targeted for the next sprint and answer any late-binding questions the team may have about them. Quite often, questions vary from specific behaviors to how the team might design and implement the feature set for the sprint.

Once phase one is finished and the team fully understands the work, they then dive-in to phase two and begin to break down each of the stories into work tasks. Keep in mind that these are ALL tasks associated with the work. For example: development, testing, design, inspections and reviews, and documentation; virtually every bit of work required to deliver the story to completion is identified by the team and the effort associated with each are estimated in hours.

So, you might ask, how does this help the customer engage? First, it fosters a view into the planning and execution dynamics of the team in order to deliver on their requests. They gain valuable glimpses into the level of difficulty and all of the work associated with each feature.

They also gain insight into the strategy the team will be using to deliver the features. Who will be working on which features and why? How is the team planning on handling dependencies and overall feature testing? How are they planning on handling risks? Also, if the team is operating as part of a larger group, how are they interacting with other teams on dependencies, integration, and collaboration?

In a word, the plans are totally transparent and open for discussion and adjustment. The team simply wants to deliver on its commitments, so constructive ideas are welcome—especially the empathy that stakeholders should realize by becoming part of the teams' planning and execution.

You see…software is rarely as simple in design or easy to construct as most bystanders believe.

Daily Stand-up

All of the agile methods have the notion of a daily team meeting for sharing progress, challenges and making real-time adjustments to the teams' work plans. In Scrum this is known as the daily Scrum and it's where stakeholders, management, and customers can gain real-time insight into the "inner workings" of their agile teams.

I remember coaching a team implementing some features in an eCommerce application. To her credit, their VP of European Operations would attend the daily stand-up meetings whenever possible while they were developing the interfaces to Amazon UK. She would listen intently to the discussions, but wouldn't interrupt the team with questions as she was a well-behaved 'Chicken' in the stand-up meeting.

However, after the more difficult conversations in many of their daily Scrums, she would pull me aside and ask questions regarding what she had 'heard' in the stand-up. Was the team in trouble? How could she help? Or, could they adjust some of their scope commitments in order to assist the team? These were very typical questions for her to ask. In some cases, her concerns were unfounded; in others, they were absolutely right on target.

The stand-up was a transparent window into the teams' work dynamics that she had never had before. No longer was she relying on written or e-mail status reports that were interpretations of progress. Now she received unfiltered, raw data from the team themselves. She encountered the highs and lows. She clearly saw the teams' challenges and, more importantly, how they approached resolving them.

She didn't need a report to tell her where the risks were. Instead, she viscerally understood them by interacting with the team. She also saw opportunities present themselves where she could assist the team by making adjustments while still achieving her overall business goals.

This was all incredibly powerful and also frightening at the same time. It enticed, encouraged, and demanded her to engage as an 'owner' with the team. To her credit, she became fully engaged and the project was ultimately a huge success.

Sprint Review or Demo

One of the core agile manifesto points is "working software over jabbering about working software"—I clearly paraphrased a bit here. You see an incredible emphasis in agile teams to discuss most of your designs, requirements, and product commentary, while looking over working software. There's literally nothing else quite like it.

In Scrum, there is a sprint review or demo ceremony at the end of each sprint. In the demo, the team is responsible for showing off their working software that was focused towards their established sprint goal(s).

This ceremony is a "Big Deal" in Scrum teams. For example, *at iContact*[2], we had sprint reviews for our teams every two weeks. These meetings were held in the largest conference room where we literally invited the entire company (yes, we were relatively small) to the event. Usually over half of our C-level team was in attendance and the room was typically standing room only.

Each team took a turn to demonstrate their efforts for the past sprint. Team members all get a shot at speaking of their efforts. The audience was fully engaged—asking questions and providing immediate feedback on the functions and features demonstrated.

Often the feedback extended beyond the demo. Attendees would follow the teams back to their office areas to provide additional feedback and/or ask to see a particular feature again. I often saw our CEO whispering his reactions to our product managers during and after the demo as he guided the vision he was personally looking for in our products.

But, beyond feedback for our teams, it shared information with our sales team, customer support group, and account managers. They become familiar with what was being developed in real-time and then could communicate those "coming attractions" directly to our customers.

It literally created "transparent knowing" across the entire company surrounding around how the product was evolving and what to expect and when.

---

[2] Chapter 8 is an expansion of the techniques used at iContact to plan, orchestrate, and adapt our Sprint Reviews.

Wrapping Up

One of the keys to engaging the customer is showing them you're listening to their feedback. That it matters to you and you'll take relatively immediate action on it. This feedback loop of:

- Listen To Feedback
- Develop & Change Software
- Demonstrate New Software
- Listen Again...

This is a wonderful device for agile teams to assure they're on the right track.

It also draws in their customers. It engages them in the process because they feel more like a partner in the teams' efforts. Not all customers will embrace this behavior. More traditional customers will be taken aback and find excuses; primarily that they don't have the time for it.

You'll need to be patient and, over time, draw them into your efforts. Working software that demonstrates solutions to your customers' most challenging problems can be...well intoxicating. So, be patient and persistent.

Agile project managers maintain their teams' focus on the heartbeat of delivering value and work hard to PULL the customer into the fray. Why? Because it's their software, they need to care, and you need their feedback. So find a way to just do it!

Thanks for listening,
Bob.

Section 2 – Execution

In many ways, the agile methods are about 'doing' software over "talking about" software—thus, the focus on 'working' software in the Agile Manifesto. In this section, I want to focus on some of the execution dynamics for agile teams. Topics include some of the harder bits that I've found teams to struggle with.

5. **Please Sir, May I Have Some Help?**
   - Seems like such a simple tenant—if you need help, ask for it--early and often. Yet, so many agile individuals, teams, and even organizations, wait far too late to reach out.
   - http://www.rgalen.com/blog/2012/6/25/the-agile-project-managerplease-sir-may-i-have-some-help.html

6. **The Triad at the Heart of Agile Collaboration**
   - The triad and the 3 amigos are just two ways to emphasize the collaboration between Developer, Tester, and Product Owner that is central to driving agile value.
   - http://www.rgalen.com/blog/2012/5/29/the-agile-project-managerthe-triad-at-the-heart-of-agile-col.html

7. **Fostering Controlled Chaos**
   - Agile isn't supposed to be so well planned out or defined, that there aren't any adjustments and learning. It's actually somewhat chaotic.
   - http://www.projecttimes.com/robert-galen/agile-project-managementcontrolled-chaos.html

8. **Voila—The Great Reveal**
   - The sprint review is the most important of the Scrum ceremonies -- part demo, part defining moment, part feedback opportunity, and part transformation agent.
   - http://www.projecttimes.com/robert-galen/the-agile-project-manager%E2%80%94voila-the-great-reveal.html

Enjoy!

5—Please sir, may I have some help?

A Sad Story

A seasoned Director of Software Development was championing agile adoption at their company. It was a moderately scaled initiative, including perhaps 100 developers, testers, project managers, BA's, and the functional management surrounding them. They received some initial agile training, seemed to be energized and aligned with the methods, and were "good to go" as they started sprinting.

Six months later things were a shambles. Managers were micro-managing the sprints while adjusting team estimates and plans. The teams were distrustful, opaque, and misleading their management. There was virtually no honest and open collaboration nor trust. They'd (re)established a very dysfunctional dance.

Funny thing is...

Their agile coach asked many times if they needed help. The answer was always..."No, things are going fine". Only when they had failed ten sprints in a row, and team members were mutinying, did the director reach out for help to their coach.

Their coach came back and in relatively short order brought the organization back to 'basics' and helped them restore balance, trust, collaboration, and commitment to agile delivery. Afterwards, everyone was asking the questions: why did it take so long and why didn't we ask for help sooner?

Another Sad Story

A set of teams in a mature internet startup had been leveraging Scrum for about 4-5 years. They were incredibly mature and were delivering well on the promises that agile has in value delivery, quality, and team morale. Things were going quite well…or, so it seemed.

But "under the covers", the teams were losing their 'edge'. Defects were on the rise. The teams weren't having impactful retrospectives and really tackling self or continuous improvement. Morale was slipping and the teams were losing their accountability towards results and value. In a word, complacency was seeping into the teams.

Funny thing is…

The organization's agile coach would have a weekly meeting with the Scrum Masters across all of the teams. She would always ask if anyone needed help, for example by attending a planning or grooming session, or by co-facilitating a retrospective, or by partnering with any Scrum Master, in coaching their teams.

That honest offer of help was never met with a request for over a year. Not even one of the experienced Scrum Masters directly asked for assistance. Instead, they mostly struggled to inspire their teams towards improvement and became comfortable, as well as defensive of the complacency trending.

A Final Sad Story

I was coaching several Scrum teams as part of a new adoption. I would count this as a true enterprise-level adoption—in that they had many teams that were starting all at once across several projects. In order to provide some coaching guidance as they began, I was rotating amongst the various team stand-ups as a 'Chicken'.

There was one team where I noticed that one of the software engineers struggling with their sprint work. In sprint planning, Sue had estimated the work to take several days to complete; really the entire team had agreed. But, as the sprint unfolded, she seemed to be struggling with the complexity of the job. On day 2 of the sprint, she identified that struggle in the stand-up, but she remained hopeful. On day 3, she was still working hard, but again, hopeful. On day 4, again…. This continued until the seventh day of the sprint when it was obvious that Sue was in trouble and the entire team tried to come and help her. Regardless of everyone's efforts, the task was attacked too late and the team failed to deliver on their sprint commitment.

Funny thing is…

This was the team's number one priority user story for the sprint. They had all committed to getting it done as part of the sprint's body of work. Yet, no one seemed interested in the fact that it was running late and jeopardizing the other work they'd committed to, as well as the overall sprint goal. That is, not until the last minute.

Beyond that, nobody on the team had asked to help her early on in the sprint, or challenged why she was struggling so, or encouraged her to ask for help.

Help Me, Where am I Going with This?

In all three of my stories there was a fundamental reluctance for people to ask for help. Not only that, when they did ask for help, it was often very late in the game and the challenge, issue, or problem was greatly exacerbated and much more difficult to tame.

The intent of this post is to explore the dynamics of this common software team anti-pattern. While it's not directly related to agile, I think it surfaces more frequently in agile teams given the self-directed, collaborative, and transparent principles the teams aspire toward.

From what I've observed in the professional landscape, it's that individuals are truly reluctant to ask for any kind of assistance. Is it ego? Is it embarrassment? Is it perfectionism? Is it trust? Is it perception? I believe it's all of these and more.

Why I'm surfacing it now is because I've been noticing it for years as part of my Agile and Scrum coaching. I see it at all levels of organizations, which my examples try to illustrate. It happens at the senior leadership level, the management level, and at the team level. It's often independent of a person's experience. Indeed, there seems to be a relationship between the more experience you have feeding your reluctance in admitting that you don't know something or need help in formulating a next step.

Some Anti-Patterns

Below is a list of some of the thought patterns I've seen exhibited within teams by people who don't want to ask for help. I know there are probably many more, but I do think this list will help to: (1) clarify the challenge or problem at hand and, (2) focus everyone towards improvement in our abilities in asking for help:

- **90% Done Syndrome**—This is when you get 90% of a project done in the first 10% of time, but the next 10% takes 90% of the remaining time. It implies that we underestimate and should assume that "finishing" a task usually takes longer than we imagine. Realizing our inherent optimism can be an inhibitor towards asking for help.

- **I've got the best skills for this specific task**—A big part of this is ego and the belief that you are the strongest link. This isn't reality and it certainly doesn't help to develop the team's overall skills either. Perhaps you could pair with someone?

- **If I want it done right, I'll do it myself; I don't trust others to do this work**—This position certainly doesn't motivate people to want to work with you. Besides, do you "always" do it right and get it done, regardless of the complexity? Probably not.

- **Everyone else is busy too** – This seems to be an empathetic and honorable approach, as long as you're making progress. However, the real question is—is everyone working on the highest priority items to meet the sprints goals? If not, or if something is delayed, then realign your efforts; it's not personal to any one person.

- **I get paid to solve problems**—No. You get paid to be a solid team member and to deliver value for your customers. No one individual has all of the answers; instead there is great power in collaboration and the wisdom of crowds. Work together as a team to solve your most challenging problems.

- **I don't want to disappoint my team**—It's not about you! Believe it or not, your team understands your strengths and weaknesses. They'll admire your effort and honesty when you ask for help when and if you're struggling.

- **I'm the only one who knows that code or understands the domain and design**—I've been here the longest and I'm the only one left with a clue about this code. Well, that will remain the situation unless you start letting others in to help you. How about mentoring your 'replacement' so you can move onto other things?

- **Don't bring me problems…bring me solutions**—This traditional management-speak was a façade to allow managers to disengage from their teams. It no longer applies. Anyone and I mean anyone that can help a team advance should be engaged to help.

- **It's embarrassing, I don't want to be the "weakest link" on our team**—I actually believe that self-aware and team-centered individuals can find a place where there are no "weak links" on a team. A place where the team covers each other's' weaknesses and simply delivers on their combined strengths.

- **I'm trying to have a "can do" or positive attitude**—I know that many engineers are infernally optimistic; however, let's also bring a healthy dose of realism and experience into play. Look at your history and be self-aware. Asking for help IS a positive response.

- **Everyone thinks I'm perfect**—I hate to break the news to you, but NO, they don't. If anyone has worked with you for any length of time, they understand your strengths AND your weaknesses -- including your inability to ask for help Therefore, be brave and raise any and all of your questions!

- **I've already started, it will take longer to hand it off to someone else**—This aligns nicely with 90% done syndrome. It's counter-intuitive and counter-productive. Teams swarming around work tend to get it done the quickest. The push here should be to ask for help and engage others as soon as you can.

- **I don't know exactly what to ask for**—The point here is that you can't ask for help until you precisely know the issue. What if you don't? How long do you wait? Asking for open-ended help is ok as long as you made honest efforts to sort things out on your own.

- **It will change everyone's perception of me**—Good! It will be a healthier, closer to reality perception. It will also be the perception that you have the maturity and the self-confidence to ask for, and hopefully offer, help within your team.

- **I'm afraid they'll "ding me" on my review**—So, what if they do? Is that really a good excuse for letting your entire team down? With your continuously improving skills, you've always got the option of moving onto a better position elsewhere.

- **This is truly a single person task**—The job is to get work done as soon as possible. Very few tasks can only be accomplished by a single "Lone Ranger". Think out of the box…and share! Once you practice swarming around work, you'll be surprised how few "single person" tasks there truly are.

In the end, all of these are simply excuses for not asking for help. We need to move away from our reluctance to ask for help and instead, embrace it.

At least from an agile team and project perspective, it's not about the individual. It's about the team. Asking for help is an acknowledgement that your team is greater than the sum of its parts, and that you have a responsibility to identify challenges and face them as a <u>team</u>.

When you're unwilling to raise them early and often, you're not seeing the big picture of collaborative team work towards a common goal.

The "Simplicity" of Agile and Coaching

One of the biggest challenges I find in my coaching is having teams ask for help. I can't tell you how often I've found that teams get a brief sense of the agile methods and dive in before they truly know what they're doing.

Part of the problem is the inherent simplicity of the methods themselves. On the surface, everything sounds so easy. All you need is:

- A self-directed team
- A customer
- A project
- A backlog (list)
- A daily stand-up
- A demo

Then life is good…right? Now that you're agile, everything will sort itself out. You simply need to keep "sprinting" and, as a result, good things will happen.

What these teams fail to grasp is that there is a huge difference in "doing Agile" vs. "being Agile". They're often focusing on the individual ceremonies, or tactics, and not truly grasping what it takes to evolve into a well-formed, mature agile team that aligns with all of the principles of agility.

Incredibly often, these "doing Agile" teams don't even realize that they've gotten off track or need help. That is, until it's quite late and there's a great deal of dysfunction in place. Or, when they realize they've failed to deliver on the results that, "being Agile", teams can produce.

They eventually reach out for a helping hand, but usually only after a whole lot of time has been wasted. As an agile project manager, don't let your team(s) fall into this trap. Remind them that agility "done well" is a complex and continuous journey and, that asking for help or getting a coach or guide, is an incredibly mature and healthy step.

How to Ask for Help?

I thought I'd just share a few words of advice in how to think about asking for help. In many ways, it's a mind-set that you have to reframe from your existing perspectives towards a new view. Here are a few thoughts on how:

Just do it! Don't think too much about it.

Keep your release, sprint and team goals in mind and be inquisitive about how the team is meeting its commitments.

It allows the team to solve their problems…not as individuals, but as a TEAM!
Never wait too long; if you "feel" like you need help…you probably do.
Remember, it's a sign of strength, not weakness.
Also, offer assistance…whenever possible…and don't always take "No" for an answer.

Pairing with each other truly aids teams in asking for help; pair often.

The retrospective is also a wonderful place to explore your personal and team growth when it comes to asking for help and working together. It should be a 'safe' environment, where solid teams reflect on their challenges and how they could have improved. One important area to continuously explore in your retrospectives is the teams' behaviors around collaborative trust and, asking for and providing, help. Try it!

Both Directions

Help is a multi-directional element. This means you'll often find yourself asking for help, and providing help, often at the same time. I think the degree to which you offer to collaborate and help will improve your own abilities in asking for and receiving help from team members.

One good way to improve is by helping your own team members; asking probing questions surrounding team challenges, and being 'real' in exchanges around getting things done.

This is particularly important at a leadership level in setting an example where asking for help is construed as a positive and normal activity within the team. Where saying "I don't know", and "Can you help me with this?" and "What do you think I should do?" are all perceived as mature, healthy, and constructive events within your organization.

I remember reading a leadership book that spoke about senior managers asking to be mentored by members of staff. The idea was that they would ask for help from people who'd been there the longest. They would also show humility and teach-ability by asking for, listening to, and digesting the wisdom these people had to offer. In doing so, they created a more collaborative and humble environment where showing vulnerability and asking for assistance was not only ok, it was the norm.

Consequently, your leadership team, leading by example and showing vulnerability, can be a key to your teams' improvement.

Wrapping Up and a Survey

In Chapter 14, we explore teams handling failure and failing. As part of that chapter, I created a short survey to poll readers to get a sense for the state of "failure acceptance" out in the real world.

The premise was that my lens might be a bit skewed and I wanted to get other perspectives. In that case, it turned out that the environment for failure acceptance was even worse than I had imagined. The results were interesting, but sad as well.

I'm inspired to try the same approach with this topic. To that end, I've created a relatively short survey surrounding organizational health (team, management, senior leadership) when it comes to asking for help. You'll find a link to it here – https://docs.google.com/spreadsheet/viewform?formkey=dDFKd1hsTTBod mUtcVRpa0hpcmJhaEE6MQ#gid=0

I would like your help in filling this out.

Wrapping this chapter up, I believe agile project managers foster an environment where asking for help is a strength and well received, where team members can embrace and welcome the opportunity to help each other out, and where they look at two-way help as being one of the strengths of their team.

The best way to start this is to lead by example. To be able to show vulnerability yourself and ask for help when the time is appropriate. To occasionally say—"I don't know" when you're dealing with daily challenges. To ask questions of the team when people appear to be struggling; encouraging them to seek help as quickly as possible.

So go ask your team to help you, and help them in asking for help…

Thanks for listening,
Bob.

References

1. http://www.businessweek.com/managing/content/jun2010/ca2010063_197398.htm
2. http://www.workhappynow.com/2012/04/how-to-ask-help-at-work/
3. http://www.nytimes.com/2011/04/10/jobs/10career.html

6—The TRIAD At The Heart Of Agile Collaboration

I was employed a few years ago at a wonderful company as an agile coach and Scrum Master. I had been spending an inordinate amount of time on the road teaching, so this local opportunity to coach a set of agile teams was timely, and incredibly welcome, by me and my family.

After joining, I was soon promoted to a Director of Software Development role and became a member of the senior leadership team. That was my title and my primary role, but I continued to coach and champion agile methods across the organization.

I used to joke about arguing with myself because I had two halves. I had the dark-side responsibility of 'management' (Darth Vader) and the light-side responsibility of 'coaching' our self-directed agile teams (Luke Skywalker). Although I felt I achieved a reasonably good balance, it certainly was challenging at times to keep my heavy breathing to a minimum.

The Triad

I was lucky in my role when I discovered two colleagues who became my partners in our agile journey. Not only were their roles central to the partnership, but we were all reasonably like-minded in our commitment to the agile methods and to creating a great team environment.

One was the Director of Quality Assurance and Testing; the other, the Director of Product Management. Including my role, this meant that we had coverage across the major functions within our technology organization including:

- Software Development and Project Management
- Quality and Product Testing
- Product Management and Marketing

We were a 'Triad' if you will.

We established a group, or committee, amongst ourselves where we focused on providing consistent leadership and guidance for our enterprise-level agile adoption. Our triad provided consistent vision, mission, and goal setting for our agile direction. To our credit, we realized early on that agile adoption wasn't only a play at the technical team level. While that level was certainly important, it also needed senior leadership understanding and support for effective steering.

Linking with the notion of Scrum of Scrums, we likened ourselves to being a Scrum of Scrums of Scrums or providing an S^3 *and* S^4 *level* [3]committee. We wanted to focus on guiding our evolution from a structural and guideline perspective, but also providing the visionary and supportive leadership that is so important to a successful agile adoption.

We discovered over time that this model worked incredibly well because most of our initiatives could never have been driven by any individual function. I'll explain more of that later by way of an example, but suffice it to say, our synergy truly mattered.

---

[3] The S3 is focused toward Portfolio Planning and the S4 towards Agile Adoption Coaching & Steering. You can read more about this in my Scrum Product Ownership book—Chapter 16.

Implications to Agile Project Management

I think the first lesson from this is that an individual function or group cannot solely drive agile adoption alone. That agility isn't simply a "collaborative game" from a team perspective. It also requires collaboration across various levels within your organization.

Organizations need to be aligned and integrated across three tiers:

- The team level themselves
- Across the middle management tier
- Across the senior leadership tier

In my example, we were operating at the senior leadership tier. We were coaching and supporting our teams. But, more importantly, we were spending a great deal of time coaching our middle management tier in their adjustments towards how to effectively lead agile teams.

From an agile project management perspective, I'm implying that your reporting / transparency, agile method's guidance, and execution leadership needs to be applied simultaneously across all three structural tiers. Perhaps not at an equal pace or velocity, but each needs to be moving forward in order for true progress to be made.

Embracing ATDD or BDD (as an example)

In order to illustrate the power of the triad in focusing on the right things, I'll use a real example.

An organizational adopting agile was supporting a Software-as-a-Service (SaaS) product suite of e-commerce applications. At one point, it was determined that the application had some significant bugs that were causing charge-backs to the company; truly costing them 'real' money.

One of the team members, a senior software developer, had the idea of leveraging Cucumber and acceptance test driven development (ATDD) or, behavior driven development (BDD), techniques as an approach to 'debug' the business logic in a specific set of transaction-control components.

Supporting the initiative

The triad came into play in the following ways as we used these testing tools and techniques first to isolate and then to repair this set of very challenging bugs:

From the Development-side

- First of all, there was the initiative shown by the individual engineer in suggesting a 'novel' and potentially risky approach to sorting out issues through some hairy legacy code while trying to solve bugs.
- This was essentially a "refactoring play"— so more courage to champion cleaning up historically messy code
- Learning new approaches and techniques can be risky and time consuming. These bugs and issues had tremendous visibility and were costing the firm 'real' revenue. So, there was outstanding visibility and pressure towards fixing them ASAP. Kudos to the team for maintaining their balance in taking the right approach.
- Finally, the development teams in this context took a whole-team view towards quality. It was everyone's job and they took that approach to initiating and delivering the repair(s).

From the Quality-side

- The quality or testing team members brought some familiarity with Cucumber to the table. They would also need to support any test automation that was created as part of this effort.
- They had to be open-minded to an automation-centric idea that was largely coming from outside the testing team.
- The testers demonstrated the solution in the sprint review. They ran the tests and needed to assure that the tests were well constructed and the test designs sound.
- They also took the ball after the demo and 'wired' these new tests into the ATDD-based regression suites so that we would catch future business logic bugs before release.

From the Product-side

- The first leap of faith here was allowing the teams to pursue "testing infrastructure" over delivering features. We needed the Product Owner to 'trust' their teams' recommendation on how to attack this problem. Given the nature of the triad, we got that.

- We also needed the product organization to run interference or cover for the team while they investigated this approach. While they might not understand what we were trying, they needed to support the approach externally... and they did.
- Finally, we needed the Product Owner to establish the correct business logic that was required. This was crucial in the test design phase. Keep in mind that in ATDD, we developed the tests first to mimic the exact business logic that was intended. Then ran the code through the tests. Starting with the correct definition of the logic helped us isolate the exceptions that were operating incorrectly.

The Delivery

With our triad-based cross team support, the team delivered a corrected product in a single sprint. At the sprint review, they identified three critical bugs that were fixed as a result of the effort. But beyond that, they identified three more unseen logic bugs that were also repaired as part of this effort. So, the business logic was thoroughly restored and now had a set of repeatable automated Cucumber tests that could be run against it whenever we wished.

We had a tough, not easily impressed, CEO at this company. But I think, (just think) I may have seen a tear come to his eye during the sprint demonstration.

Wrapping Up

I hope my example illustrated to you the necessity for and power of the triad in agile teams. It's much harder (or even impossible) for an individual function to initiate continuous improvement change by themselves.

Instead, you need the power of collaboration via the triad model of (Development + Quality + Product) to share perspectives and fully deliver on the promises of agility. This isn't only at the team level, but is important at all levels within your organization.

As an agile project manager, you'll want to focus on triad-based interactions at all levels within your team and organization. Always reinforce whole-team solutions and collaboration, while also discouraging silo-based thinking as much as possible. Remember, agile adoption is not "a technology only based methodology" play, but instead is an "organization-wide transformation" play.

By taking this broader view, you'll deliver better solutions with your teams. Go Triad!

Thanks for listening,
Bob.

Reference Post-script

I've leveraged the idea of the Triad as an organizational collaboration model. However, it's often used to illustrate the agile team collaboration model that helps define, refine and deliver on customer requirements.

1. Ken Pugh has written a wonderful book that speaks directly to this 'Triad' of Developer + Tester + Product Owner. It entitled: Lean-Agile Acceptance Test-Driven Development: Better Software Through Collaboration.
2. Gojko Adzic has written another book that focuses in this same space. While not directly referencing "the Triad", it provides additional insights into collaboration around specifications. It's entitled: Specification by Example: How Successful Teams Deliver the Right Software.
3. George Dinwiddie has written about it with a slightly different label. He speaks about the 3 Amigos, but it's essentially the same topic and point – http://www.stickyminds.com/sitewide.asp?Function=edetail&ObjectType=COL&ObjectId=17232&tth=DYN&tt=siteemail&iDyn=2

In both of these cases, the triad is driving collaboration towards building what the client truly needs that solves their real challenges and problems. Both are highly recommended. Like I said earlier…Go Triad!

7—Fostering Controlled Chaos

As you may or may not know, I'm an active agile coach. I often get asked to enter new teams and jump-start them or assess an existing teams' overall level of agile-ness. One of the factors that I look for in a strong and healthy agile team is what I'll call _controlled chaos_.

You see, the atmosphere in these teams isn't safe nor predicted too far in advance. The teams don't have a false sense of security. They're working on a short list of features in close collaboration with their Product Owner. They know that challenges will rise up to meet them. Risks will fire. Team members will get sick, get married, or tend to ill parents. The design approaches and the code won't always work as advertised.

They may or may not have the technical skills to interface with the new third party vendor you've just signed an agreement with. They also struggle mightily to deliver software of sufficient quality, scratch that; they struggle to deliver solid software—even though they focus on it daily.

What I'm trying to say is that in these dynamic teams…"Stuff Happens". Plans shift daily and the team must respond to this landscape. To be undeterred in their commitments to sprint and release goals and to be creative and relentless in attacking impediments. Agile project managers need to understand this chaotic reality—in fact, they need to create, foster and embrace it! Next we'll explore a few ideas on how to do that.

Don't Ask for Specific Commitments

Imagine yourself in a canoe on a river you've never navigated before. You have a map, so you know generally where you're going. You have a GPS, so you know specifically where you are. Now, you get an emergency call from your boss and he/she wants to know _exactly_ when you'll arrive at the take-out location. What do you say?

From my point-of-view, there's very little you can say. You simply don't know how long it will take. You can guess and give your boss a sense of comfort OR you can tell him/her the truth. I'm here and my hourly rate appears to be this. My map implies the following obstacles and journey length. I think I may get there sometime between 4-7 pm depending on conditions.

A key here is that in highly variable and complex situations, we often don't have a very clear idea of how long something will take. Instead, we need to _triangulate_ to get to our destination. We'll take daily samples of progress, looking ahead on our journey and then reducing the uncertainty as we gain knowledge, make progress, and get closer to our goal.

That's the reality of complex systems. Therefore, the question for an effective agile project manager becomes, do you want the truth, with incremental triangulation, or a façade of absolute certainty? I think we need to emphasize the integrity of the former and support it with active team focus, high communication and collaboration, as well as, full transparency.

The key points being—leave the façade for those who _can't handle the truth_.

Don't Allow the Team to Plan Too Far in Advance

There's a planning technique used in agile teams called release planning. You see it referenced in a few different methods with slightly different names:

- In Extreme Programming it's referred to as the **Planning Game**
- Scrum and Jim Highsmith refer to it as **Release Planning and Agile Project Management** techniques
- The Crystal methodology refers to it as **Blitz Planning**
- Likewise, Jeff Patton has championed a technique of planning stories from a customer usage perspective called **Story Mapping**

All of these techniques are focused towards establishing a high level, end-to-end view of your project, leading towards a planned release point. It turns out that they're all incredibly useful for envisioning where your project is 'going'. For instance, let's say providing the map in my earlier canoe example.

The danger comes when you start performing detailed planning (tasking, dependency mapping, detailed design, etc.) too far in advance. You, as well as the team, will get a false sense of comfort believing that you know where you're going. However, along the way, there will be rapids and nasty weather that will surely knock you off course.

Trying to fully anticipate them is mostly a fool's errand and can be very wasteful of your time. Being prepared for them, and reacting quickly when you encounter them, is the way to go. You'll want to plot out a fair distance in your planning, but not too far, and you'll also want to stay out of the micro-details.

The best strategy is to first pull a high-level release plan together as a team. Then complete several sprints and compare your results (plans, velocity, capacity, etc.) against your release plan. Then re-plan your release, with potentially shifting scope as your primary means to triangulate towards a date target.

Continue this oscillation between high-level planning and low-level execution and discovery until you meet your release goals or your destination. Then rinse and repeat for the next release or trip.

General Guidance for "Look–Ahead" Timing

In my own teams I share a heuristic for this balance between high level planning and low level execution details. It surrounds the following:

<u>Do end-to-end, release planning for your current release only! Then, complete it before 25% of your release execution has occurred.</u>

- *Keep your User Stories mostly at an Epic level before release sequence entry, but early on in the release, refine them to well-sized or sprint executable user stories.*

<u>Proximity for Sprint or Iteration look-ahead:</u>

- *Have your next 2-3 sprints (in User Stories relatively well defined – towards 80% clarity); Beyond that, the Backlog is mostly high-level Epics.*

- *Have your next release (User Stories) planned at an Epic level; when your within 1-2 sprints of your current release and beginning the next release. Within 1 sprint of the new release, start to do more granular decomposition—getting ready for your next round of Release Planning.*

Always remember that backlog grooming is an iterative process that needs continuous attention. These tend to guide teams towards the right level of look-ahead and appropriate granular planning.

Don't Write Everything Down

I want to shift gears a bit and talk about documentation. Historically, we've used documentation to combat the chaos—thinking that if we write down all the details of our plans, designs, and agreements, they won't change. That same logic applied to our canoe trip might be catastrophic if we encountered a storm.

Regarding project requirements and other project artifacts, you'll want to apply the 80:20 rule or Pareto Principle in here. I would contend that only the most important parts of the project need recording. Serious design elements, important bugs, retrospective results, user stories or other agile requirements, acceptance tests, are good examples of what might fall into this category.

As a heuristic, try to influence your team to record only 20% of the things that they would normally try to record. Guide them towards the more important artifacts, while trimming out the excess or waste. You know the ones, usually driven by some process checklist or the team's false desire to leave more legacy details than anyone will ever read.

The other rationale here is that software changes…quickly. Consequently, information surrounding it has a very short half-life and decays just as quickly. You'll want to ensure that you are keeping the most important bits up-to-date and with that comes a cost.

Turning it around, another heuristic is to only target 70-80% completeness of your user stories prior to their execution. We never want fully vetted, 100% defined, little/no ambiguity, stories hitting our teams; stories where everyone looks around and assumes they have a "complete understanding". When that occurs, conversation and collaboration stops within the sprint, which is the enemy of agile requirements.

In both of these situations, agile project managers take on the role of fighting for ambiguity in documentation. You should fight for terseness, for just-in-time, just-enough thinking and collaboration within your teams.

You want to hear lots of conversations. Heated debates around a particular feature and lots of discussion surrounding quality. Your first and second levels of documentation surround the code, the tests, and the stories—so, keep your priorities focused there. You want clarity to be achieved, not in planning or at the beginning of an iteration, that's too soon. Instead, you want clarity to result from collaborative execution and delivery of completed stories within each sprint.

You see, ultimate clarity comes at the end of agile iterations—when we demonstrate a user story to our customer and they say YES, that's exactly what I was looking for.

Wrapping Up

Wrapping up, healthy agile teams need to be uncomfortable, leaning into the unknown, and tense with anticipation. They need to be on the edge of chaos with just-enough clarity to get their canoe to the next segment in the river. Along with an eye towards impediments and risks that might be right around the corner.

In a word, they need to be agile and adaptive. Great agile project managers continuously foster this environment within their teams, looking to stay on the hairy edge of chaos. They don't push too hard for data or commitments when the team's state isn't close enough to warrant it. They truly understand the notion of triangulating towards a goal and maintaining a healthy balance between "the known", "the documented", and the "the chaos".

Now, doesn't that sound like fun? Thanks for listening,
Bob.

8—Violà: The Great Reveal

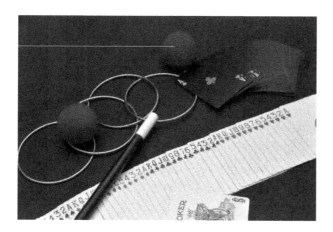

I remember this day as if it was yesterday. It was my first sprint review at a company I'd just joined as an agile coach. They'd been 'doing' Scrum for several years and I had gotten the general sense that they were very well disciplined and mature agilists.

So, when they scheduled a series of sprint reviews to expose the x-team efforts of their latest sprint cycle, I was understandably excited. I got into the room early to get a good seat and was eager with anticipation.

Gradually, the room filled up and it became quite noisy, which only drove my anticipation higher. At that time, the first team took "the stage" and began their review. They popped up some PowerPoint slides and away they went…

Their slide deck was polished. They had lists of things they'd done and down-loaded pictures and jokes for lightening the mood at appropriate points. They marched through the work that they'd done…one slide at a time, and at appropriate points, the audience politely applauded their approval.

However, it struck me mid-way through the first review that something was missing—something really, really important. There was no working software. I wondered how this could be. The whole point of the sprint review was to expose working code to stakeholders for review and feedback. Then I thought, this was probably an exception or special case specific to just this team. Surely there's working software coming up next.

But, one-by-one, each subsequent team followed the same pattern; showing humorous slides and textual representations of effort, but no working code to be seen. Slowly, and then more quickly, my enthusiasm waned and I became quite frustrated. Not so much with the team, but with whoever had explained the purpose of a sprint review to everyone. Clearly…they just didn't "get it" and neither did the stakeholders. They continued to politely chuckle at jokes and applaud each of the teams' efforts. However, it seemed as if the ceremony was simply there to check a box in the Scrum process list.

Never Again!

Needless to say, the teams never quite took this same approach again in their sprint reviews. While I truly honor the notion of self-directed teams, I immediately laid out some prescriptive guidelines and clear goals for our future sprint reviews.

Some of them aligned quite naturally with the Agile Manifesto. For example, the notion of demonstrating working code at the end of each iteration or sprint. But, some of the guidelines were unique to our organizational and cultural dynamics.

That's actually the focus of this chapter…I want to share some of the guidelines, strategies, and the mindset we leveraged to turn-around our sprint reviews. Over time we moved from:

- Polite applause ..to.. enthusiastic cheers and "Aha" moments
- Polite applause ..to.. gaining congruent and constructive feedback
- Selling and marketing our results ..to.. making them transparently open to scrutiny
- Small crowds ..to.. standing room only and video taping
- PowerPoint's ..to.. working software <u>whenever possible</u>
- Entertainment ..to.. showing business value and exposing teams challenges and efforts
- Going through the motions ..to.. gaining intentional and congruent feedback

- Selling and marketing our results ..to.. having them speak for themselves!

Surely, it didn't happen overnight; we continued to adjust and fine-tune our sprint reviews over time. However, we achieved a state in our reviews where they became the cornerstone for our agile adoption across the organization.

Let me share some of the things we focused towards…

Guidance towards "Excellent" Sprint Reviews

In general, I like to consider the sprint review as a "Big Deal". Why? Because it is.

An agile team has spent a focused period of time, working on the most important stories on the planet, and is ready to deliver working software surrounding those features or stories. This stuff is hot off the presses and people should inherently care. They should be excited to see the results. Heck, you should have to beat them away at the doors.

It's the team's responsibility to effectively <u>reveal</u> their efforts. And I'm not simply talking about the software. No, they should be telling and showing a story surrounding their work. It should contain context and narrative and, there should be a connection to the last sprint and towards future sprints.

Below I want to share some critical focus points and a sample review agenda for your consideration. I hope the specific ideas will help you to improve your reviews, more effectively engage your stakeholders, and create a more <u>energetic reveal</u> for your teams.

7 Key Focus Points for Your Sprint Reviews

1. **Ownership**

   We established that the Product Owner 'owns' the overall pattern for the Sprint Review. Sure, it's a "whole team" thing but, at the end of the day, external communication, showing planned vs. delivered value, as well as, gathering and adjusting to feedback are primary aspects of the Product Owner role. They're also responsible for getting people in the review—so, if attendance is spotty, they've got work to do to figure out why and to change your patterns to get the "right people" in the room.

   Very often I think of their role as Master of Ceremony—where they are *conducting* all aspects of the review. Certainly not doing everything themselves, but guiding the overall quality, focus, and results of the review.

2. **Format**

   We put a lot of thought into the scheduling and timing for the review (or reviews if you're part of a multi-team initiative). You'll want to get into a regular tempo (day and time) for your reviews. Within the context of the review, you'll want each team to follow a consistent flow (see potential review agenda template below).

   In our case, we had multiple teams demoing on the same day—as our sprints were synchronized. Our format was really a cross-team agenda that sliced a 3-hour time slot into appropriate stages for each team. Not only did we plan each review, but our Chief Product Owner took an active role in planning or conducting the overall review flow across the teams.

3. **Sprint Goals**

   I prefer the view where the review is "hinged" on the sprint goal(s) that the team(s) signed up for. Quite often, I tell teams when they're crafting their goals to think about the e-mail invitation they'll be sending out for the reviews. Another way of crafting the sprint goal is like an "elevator pitch" or other short and descriptive analogy. The 'story' of the sprint then is tied to the goal and how the team adjusted towards meeting that goal.

Also, you should be honest about how the team delivered to their sprint commitments, so "Call It" as a success or failure. But never, ever use the term 'failure' to browbeat the team. Failure is a part of team's learning and the organization needs to *adopt a "fail forward"* [4]attitude.

4. **Whole Team View**

As I mentioned earlier, I like the view where the Product Owner is the Master of Ceremonies, the Scrum Master is the facilitator (if needed), and the entire team gets a chance to "show off" their results in each review. This whole-team approach serves to give your team transparency and the chance to shine—so round-robin your demo presenters and give everyone (person, role, etc.) a chance to show off their work and results.

However, don't 'force' introverts to speak uncomfortably in a large forum. Make it encouraged and optional. Very often these folks can serve as the 'driver' for the demo—so quietly participate. But, make sure to engage the whole team!

5. **Preparation**

If there's a key to a solid sprint review its preparation—somewhere safely between "way too much" and "totally winging it". You should put some thought into what work is relevant for the review, in what flow should it be demonstrated, as well as, how it connects to previous and upcoming sprint work.

Quite often someone with a QA background will develop a review 'script' that helps the team expose their efforts in a cohesive way. Ultimately, the Product Owner should have the strongest voice into what gets exposed and why—setting the stage for the 'reveal' with the stakeholders.

If in doubt, reserve sufficient time in sprint planning for review preparation and DO prepare.

---

[4] In Chapter 14 we discuss failure in more detail and this John Maxwell viewpoint of "Failing Forward" as a positive or constructive posture.

6. **Execution and Demonstration**

The review demo needs to be smooth, thoughtful, polished, and ultimately—the software needs to flawlessly work. Dry-running the demo and having everything pre-setup is a must. You should also perform timings to ensure that your demos fit into your allotted time. Also, don't forget about Q&A time.

Beyond the demo, you need to tell a story that encompasses your feature workflows. I've seen teams in their first sprint show an architectural diagram that reflected the work they planned for the upcoming six sprints. Then in each sprint review, they "filled in the boxes" as they began fleshing out the application architecture. I thought this approach was an outstanding way to "connect the dots" for the audience.

From my perspective, ALL WORK that a team took on in a sprint is a candidate for exposure. That might include: features, enhancements, bug fixes, refactoring, documentation, testing infrastructure, virtually everything. Sure, some things might require some finesse to demonstrate or illustrate, but if it's work the team did—it's a candidate for the review.

However, do teams need to demonstrate every bit or work they completed? I think not. I'd rather have the Product Owner and team collaborate on the most meaningful flow that illustrates their accomplishments towards their sprint goal commitment. But don't get stuck in "feature only" demonstrations.

Finally, be ready to explain things sufficiently so your audience UNDERSTANDS what you've just shown; its significance, as well as, the level of effort behind it.

7. **Wrap-up**

We've always wrapped up reviews with a general request for feedback—both on the software itself, but also on our review dynamics. Were the transitions well made? Did we explain what we did? Do you know how to send us your feedback, and what can we change to make the next review even better?

We usually only spend a few minutes here, but it's time well spent. If you're familiar with the notion of a <u>Fist-of-Five</u>, we usually leveraged that technique for closing feedback.

Sample Meeting Agenda

Consider the following as a healthy template for your team's sprint review agenda—

1. **Introduction**
2. **Team Chart**
   - who's-who: names, roles, and location of team members
   - external folks who helped with the sprint
3. **Acknowledgements – Appreciations**
   - certainly shout-outs for team members
   - but also a good time to recognize "external folks" who were instrumental in the sprint
4. **Sprint Goal**
   - articulate the Sprint Goal, speak to any adjustments that were made during the sprint
   - call it: was the sprint a success, i.e., did the team meet their commitment to the sprint goal?
5. **Strategy? Success? Efforts? Discoveries? Results?**
   - share any relevant strategies the team used to deliver the work
   - explore the effort behind the sprint
   - were there any discoveries that were unexpected; any critical results
   - all of this is to give the audience a "behind-the-scenes" look at the team's sprint
6. **Demo's; Q&A**
   - demo the selected set of user stories / features – allow for Q&A
7. **Coming Attractions**
   - speak to progress to release goal(s) and upcoming work in future sprints
8. **Fist-of-Five Towards Improvement**
   - engage the audience in review performance feedback
9. **Close**

Wrapping Up

I simply can't tell you how good it feels to have a high-impact sprint review. While I put a lot of pressure on the Product Owner and team for the results of the review, as an agile project manager, you play a central role as well.

Teams often get "caught up" in the work of the sprint and short-shrift the review preparation. In fact, this is a common anti-pattern. You can turn this around in sprint planning—asking the team to plan for and allocate sufficient time towards the review, while also reminding them as the end of the sprint approaches to consolidate their work.

Remember, the review is also a "QA checkpoint" for the team. There's nothing like pulling things together and demoing them to bring a healthy dose of reality to a team's sprint efforts. You always shake things out: environments that aren't working, integrations that weren't made, and interactions that were forgotten.

So, Agile Project Managers, I hope this post has inspired you to take charge of your sprint reviews and make them the most powerful event within your agile teams. While it is certainly the team's responsibility to prepare and deliver, you can influence the attitude and approaches. You can also amplify the positive feedback you'll get as you improve.

Thanks for listening,
Bob.

BTW: A presentation of this material was shared at the 2012 Atlanta Scrum Gathering. You might find it interesting as it compliments this article – http://www.rgalen.com/presentation-download/presentations/Dynamic%20Sprint%20Reviews%20-%20Stories%20%20Techniques.pdf

Section 3 – Customer

If you study anything related to the agile methods, you'll see an incredibly strong focus on solving customer problems and providing them value. In many ways, agile teams are totally dependent on their customers for workflow via delivering Product Backlogs. In this section we explore the dynamics of well-defined backlogs and the part that customers, Product Owners, and stakeholders play in driving it within their teams.

9. Driving Value or Where's the Beef?
- Determining product value is incredibly important with agile teams, as they always focus on priority-based (value) delivery. Here we explore some aspects of determining value.
- http://www.projecttimes.com/robert-galen/agile-project-managementdriving-value-or-wheres-the-beef.html

10. Product Backlogs: Boulders, Rocks, and Pebbles
- Teams struggle with decomposition in their backlogs. Here is an analogy with examples that should help.
- http://www.batimes.com/robert-galen/product-backlogs-boulders-rocks-and-pebbles%E2%80%A6oh-my.html

11. Product Backlogs: Mature Ownership of Agile Product Backlogs
- There's the view that the Product Backlog is simply a prioritized list of features. That's wrong. Here's we'll explore the nuance of a mature and well-balanced Product Backlog.

12. Product Backlogs: Grooming Checklist & Smells
- Ken Schaber recommend 10% of a team's time be spent in backlog preparation (grooming). Here we explore the dynamics of that practice.
- http://www.batimes.com/robert-galen/grooming-your-agile-backlogs-for-success.html

Enjoy!

9—Driving Value Or Where's The Beef?

There was a wonderful commercial I remember from years ago where a matronly woman named Clara Peller judged hamburgers by the amount of beef she found in them. Quite often, when she was disappointed in her quest, she would shout "Where's the Beef?" in frustration. Wendy's was the chain who came up with the advertising idea and to this day the line has become a catch-phrase for value delivery and customer expectations.

I guess Clara was onto something though. In my experience, businesses often miss the 'Beef' when they're trying to deliver value to their customers—particularly in the software product arena. I don't know why that is exactly. Sometimes I think the developers are too distanced from their customers. They can rarely touch or observe them or understand their true business challenges. So they're guessing when it comes to needs—more or less throwing the software "over the wall" for feedback.

Quite often teams are under the gun to deliver a smorgasbord of features. Almost as if no one knows what the customer needs, so they shotgun scatter individual features hoping to ultimately hit the customer's needs—fingers crossed. While this may be somewhat successful, it also results in delivering low to no value features that dilute the focus of the team and increase product development costs. From my perspective, nothing could be more wasteful.

Wouldn't it be wonderful if we could focus entirely on "The Beef" in application development? Spending most of our energy focused on delivering high-value and high-need solutions to our customers. Cutting through the clutter of disappointment and ambiguity and simply working on what matters most?

While it sounds like a fairy tale, the agile methods aspire to just this purpose. But it's not easy to achieve and the effective Agile Project Manager plays a wonderful role in this quest. In this chapter, I want to share some ideas on how to focus the team towards just such value delivery.

Fingers crossed…

A Prioritized Backlog!

One of the first mechanisms that drive value is the Product Backlog—the simple prioritized list that defines what an agile team builds. Every team should be laser focused on prioritizing their backlogs in numerical (1..n) order. There can't be three or four priority one features—there can be only one; then a two, a three, and so on.

Trust me. Your customers and stakeholders will want to play infinite games with priority.

I've seen cases where they have groupings in a spreadsheet that are prioritized along with sub-features broken out within each of them. They'll insist that they can't decompose the value out any further as they try to overload priority. This (1a, 1b,..1z) approach allows them to escape true prioritized decision-making, also indicating their innate inability to make hard choices regarding what's truly most important.

Don't let them do that!

An effective product backlog is always in linear and clear priority order. The team should always deliver the highest priority features first. They will work on them first and finish them first, ensuring the customer is engaged as appropriate in their development. They'll also achieve customer sign-off or acceptance of each story before they move onto others.

Since the customer is the final arbiter of priority, they shouldn't really complain about this approach. It's simply that we've historically allowed them to give us incredibly large lists of features without making finely grained priority distinctions—so they've gotten a bit lazy.

When encouraged (forced) to prioritize, I've never seen a stakeholder who couldn't make relative priority decisions; even though they might be hard and complex decisions.

Customer-Driven Value

Prioritization can also be driven by perceived value—change that to should be driven. One technique used by many agile teams is the notion of playing value poker. It's a variation of the planning poker technique made popular by Mike Cohn that is used for user story size estimation. But instead of determining size of stories in story points, we use value points as the determinant of a user story or features value to the business—it's *value priority* if you will.

One variation of the technique is to use a deck of cards labeled from 1—10, one being the lowest value and ten the highest. Keeping things simple, you can actually just label 3x5 cards with the numbers. For each user story or theme/collection of stories, you will ask a group of various customers and stakeholders to 'vote' on their thoughts towards story value.

They should all vote at once. Once the vote is complete, you take a round-robin approach discussing the 'why' behind the highest and lowest values—letting the customers and stakeholders express their nuanced views towards value. It's this rich discussion across value variance that is what you want to foster.

Once the discussion is over, you re-vote and re-discuss until you narrow the value as much as possible. Sometimes you gain agreement across the stakeholders on a common value. Sometimes you simply get a range of values, therefore, capture the specific value or the range and move on.

You might even categorize values from the different perspectives of the participants. For example, the quality and testing folks might value a particular story as a five, while the business folks value it as a three and development, or technology folks, as a one. All of these specific valuations provide important data as to how you cross-functionally value the feature. Clearly this spread would generate some meaningful discussion across the functional perspectives of team members.

This logic might be applied to multiple stakeholders as well. For example, the North American stakeholders might value a feature at six, while the EMEA stakeholders think it only a three. In all of these cases, discussing VALUE as a distinct attribute helps everyone in effective prioritizing. But beyond that, it gives hints on how much fit and finish or effort to apply to individual features.

A Variation—You Have a 'Budget' to Spend

An effective variation on the value poker technique is to give every voting or contributing partner a 'pool' of funding to spend as part of their voting. So not only are they voting on a value, but they have to invest a portion of their fixed budget or pool of dollars on the feature as well.

Quite often monopoly money, or a similarly fun equivalent, is used for this purpose. For example, let's say everyone gets $5,000 to spend on their features as we play priority poker. In one particular case, a business stakeholder votes a nine for a feature.

In order to emphasize the importance, they put up $1,500 on the feature, or about 30% of their available funds. In fact, they only spend their pool against a total of seven features. While they continue to prioritize subsequent features, they've clearly communicated their views towards value. In fact, that $1,500 feature ends up being the #1 priority story with a total value pool of $12,000 across the entire voting team OR 25% of the total available pool.

Here's an interesting question. If you're implementing this story, what does #1 Priority convey vs. #1 Priority AND 25% of the project value pool? From my perspective, there's a large difference. This feature is a much more significant portion of the value and requires particular care in collaborative definition, execution, and ultimate delivery. I hope you see a difference as well.

Now, let's review a few more ways to think about what's most valuable when prioritizing product backlogs.

Minimal Marketable Feature (MMF) or

Minimal Marketable Product (MMP)

Often in agile teams, singular stories don't have sufficient mass or impact to effectively be VALUE-ated by the team or customer. Earlier I spoke in terms of themes of stories. This is a common way of bundling stories together that have value and meaning as a collection. Not only does it help in developing sets of meaningful functionality, but if you prioritize at the thematic or collection level, it greatly simplifies your prioritization. It also has more meaning from the customers' perspective—since they tend to think in terms of features or workflows and not the more granular stories.

A variation on this theme (pun intended) is the Minimal Marketable Feature/Product or MMF/MMP. This concept originated in the Kanban and Lean communities. Essentially, it's the same as a theme, but it brings to bear the notion of deliverability, marketability, and overall customer usage.

Quite often an MMF/P is larger than a theme. It could be equivalent to a user story epic and require many sprints and/or teams to complete. However, once completed, the team will usually physically deliver the MMF/P to the customer—for example, pushing it into a production environment.

MMF Driving Synchronization and Clarity

Recently, I've been coaching teams that are struggling with their focus. There's an anti-pattern that affects many teams where they start sprinting before they understand the business case and intent for their release(s). They're delivering stories, but they don't necessarily understand the minimal set of functionality that their customers are looking for.

Not having this clearly articulated up-front becomes a fundamental problem for them. Quite often their customers have an expectation of delivery that is quite different from what the team is sprinting towards delivering. Consequently, there's no collaborative clarity around what the MMF or MMP is between the team and the stakeholder.

One nice way to connect the two back together is to establish a view towards the releases' MMF. Part of defining the MMF is the round-trip discussions that occur as the teams estimate and/or size up the stories within the MMF. The customer reevaluates whether they truly need that functionality given the investment of time. This collaboration dove-tails quite nicely into release planning—as the team narrows into fitting the MMF into a specific release window.

I've even seen multiple sorts of MMF's developed for release planning—for example, a UX MMF that tries to capture usability and interaction flows vs. the cost of implementing them. Or, similarly, an Architecture / Refactoring MMF that tries to guide these sorts of trade-offs.

I consider an MMF to be a necessary component of *agile project chartering* [5] and release planning and develop them as part of any significantly sized or scoped agile projects.

MMF or MMP Simplicity

When a team is defining their minimal marketable feature or product, I want it to fit on a single sheet of paper. I'm looking for the elevator pitch or 'essence' of the product to be described.

I often ask for what needs to be in the product to be defined, but also what doesn't need to be in the product. Occasionally, I use this "what's in vs. what's out" chart to get the point across. It defines the must haves and the must not haves for the MMF (or MMP). It turns out the crucial part of the chart is the gray area in between these two dimensions and the discussions that surround understanding the *minimal set of functionality* [6].

Often features will move back and forth. Features will get broken down and some aspects move from one column or the other or they are removed entirely. Let me give you an example to help illustrate this concept. If we were doing a simple collaborative white-boarding tool for agile teams, the following might be a reasonable MMP definition to start discussions across your team.

---

[5] In fact, in Chapter 3 we discuss the critical aspects of Agile Chartering. The notions if Minimal Marketable and Viable features and products are crucial to that exercise.

[6] It turns out that organizations and teams truly struggle with focusing on a Must Have set of functionality. The MMx construct helps quite a lot in keeping the focus…minimal.

MMF Must Have (Black)	Collaborative Grey Area	MMF Will Not Have (White)
• Visual swim lanes – vertical & horizontal • Create notes (colors) • Drag & drop notes • Shape library • Drawing tool • Multiple users collaborate on a board • Save/recall a board • Identify board participants • Default boards for Scrum & Kanban		• Board item export • Any integration with other tools • Cut & paste • Save in common file formats • Interact with board users directly (ex: text or comment) • Performance doesn't matter

I hope the example helped to illustrate the concept.

Caution: There is Minimum. Then there is Viable

There's a wonderful Harvard Business Review blog article where David Aycan discusses additional nuances associated with the notion of an MMF. He makes the point that quite often today, in our fervor to hit the 'minimum', we over-simplify features and products and lose customer and business viability.

I haven't seen this pattern that much myself; I usually see the reverse, or teams incessantly trying to build "too much". But, he connects it to Eric Ries's Lean Startup work and I have been around enough people who are passionate about those ideas that I can see it happening. Regardless, I'd recommend you read his post.

I think the key is for us to focus on Minimal and Viable as much as possible when we're framing reactions to our customers' needs.

Finally, a Trip to MoSCoW

MoSCoW prioritization is a technique for breaking requirements (or Stories & Features) down into four specific categories for consideration, discussion, and execution. They are:

- **Must Haves** – will not release without these features and capabilities being present
- **Should Haves** – high priority features
- **Could Haves** – moderate priority, fit if time allows, but deferrable
- And **Won't Haves** – features negotiated out of this release for now

When prioritizing your backlog, it helps to place these four 'buckets' on a wall or table and to visually discuss and move stories around from one to the other.

Many groups come up with some sort of ratio that helps with this. For example, out of 100 stories, perhaps only 10-20% should effectively be Must Haves and 20-30% might be valid Should Haves. This gives you some general guidance on how to compose stories into an MMF or, more often, an MMP definition.

You might want to try Moscow as a facilitative technique when you're prioritizing. My experience is that it helps to drive discussion and encourages the team to wrestle with truly "must haves" versus everything else.

Tracking Value

One of the wonderful additions to your tool-set as an agile project manager is burning down (or up) the value of stories, themes, MMF's or MMP's. You'll want to setup a burnup chart in a well-visited location that burns up team-delivered value. As with all burnup charts you'll want to encourage everyone to focus on progress while interacting with the teams.

Normally you will calculate value at a release level—setting up your burnup on an iteration-by-iteration basis.

If you're getting healthy agile behavior within your teams, you'll see value being delivered in a front-loaded fashion. You should also see healthy done-ness and quality attributes as these high-value features are delivered. In fact,

I usually expect teams to factor in value as part of their overall quality and testing strategies.

Wrapping Up

Agile Project Managers don't just care about by-rote execution of tasks or stories. No! Instead, they focus their teams on a multi-faceted and nuanced view towards customer value-driven execution. They do this by partnering with the Product Owner and the team(s) and crafting views (clearly and well written stories and features, MMFs, MMPs, and Moscow prioritization) that help the team envision their direction.

Not only are they hoping to deliver value first, but they're also hoping that by doing so, the customer may achieve a "good enough" view towards incrementally delivered product increments. This will enable the team to stop the project earlier than planned or expected. Stopping after delivering the features and functionality that truly matters the most to their customers.

It's this sort of value-trimming that can truly make an agile team stand-out from their traditional counterparts and move so much faster. That is if stakeholders step out of their comfort zone and truly focus on value first.

Thanks for listening,
Bob.

References

Here are a few useful references for the planning poker and valuation techniques.

1. http://www.agile42.com/cms/pages/business-value-game/
2. http://agilesoftwaredevelopment.com/blog/peterstev/figuring-out-business-value-planning-poker
3. http://www.allaboutagile.com/prioritization-using-moscow/
4. MMF and MMP - http://www.agilebok.org/index.php?title=Minimally_Marketable_Feature_%28MMF%29
5. Moscow - http://en.wikipedia.org/wiki/MoSCoW_Method
6. David Aycan blog - http://blogs.hbr.org/cs/2012/05/dont_let_the_minimum_win_over.html

10—Product Backlogs: Boulders, Rocks, And Pebbles...Oh My!

One of the hardest things to do in agile requirements is to break things down into constituent parts for execution. I use the term <u>backlog grooming</u> to represent this activity. There are a couple of key factors to it. First, is the notion that you can't (or shouldn't) break everything down at once into small components of work.

Truly, it's not that you can't. In traditional projects we almost always break things down into small, more granular pieces. That's not that hard. What's difficult is doing it without any knowledge of the real-world aspects of the work, since you haven't done any yet.

In agile projects, you work from a product backlog or a list of features, to-do lists, and activities, that are all focused towards completing a project. The list is in priority order and is executed in that order. Although not all elements of the list are defined at the same level of clarity or granularity. Why? Because it can often be a waste of time as you revisit the backlog often; completing bits and pieces of the work/project as you make progress.

My analogy is that a solid backlog consists of different sizes of user stories. There are boulders, rocks, and pebbles. Pebbles are finely grained stories that are ready for the very next sprint—i.e. high priority items. As priority decreases, the size of the stories increases—from rocks to boulders. In this chapter, I want to explore the dynamics of these three levels of size for handling product backlogs represented by user stories.

Boulders

Let's start out with an example of a boulder. The project in this case is a word processor—something we're all generally familiar with. Call it Microsoft Word or Google Docs.

The boulder-level story is:

> *As a writer, I want to format text in a wide variety of fashions, so that I can highlight different levels of interaction with my readers.*

That's the description of the story itself. As you know, solid stories contain acceptance tests as well. Would you even create acceptance tests at this level? I probably wouldn't, but the choice is yours.

Now, if this was in a list of related boulders, we wouldn't work on it very much or very often, particularly if it was a lower priority. But, what if this was a relatively high priority boulder and your Product Owner wanted us to get some traction on it? What would be the next step?

Rocks

I'd say break it down into rocks. In this case, these would still be rather large user stories. They would be ambiguous and their priority would be fluid. So, what's the value in breaking them down?

Mostly so that we can start to visualize the various parts of the boulder and decide which rocks to tackle first versus which rocks might be deferred to later. Here are some example rocks pulled from our example boulder:

1. *As a writer, I want to allow for text font changes; 20-30 different font types, colors, so that I can highlight different levels of interaction with my readers*

2. *…Allow for various attributes: underline, bolding, sub/super script, italicize, etc…*
3. *Allow for a form of headings; 3 primary levels*
4. *Allow for indenting of text*
5. *Allow for lists (numbered and bulleted); single level first, then move to multi-level*
6. *Allow for alignment – right/left justified, centered, variable*
7. *Allow for do/un-do to include ongoing text activities*
8. *Establish a paragraph model (or a variety of models)*
9. *Show/hide 'hidden' formatting marks*
10. *Establish the notion of a "style set" that can be used to establish a collection of favorites*

I'll stop now, but we could clearly go on and on with this exercise; I think this is a nice set of rock-level user stories for an initial discussion. These are essentially ready for backlog grooming with the team. Keep in mind that some of them border on being boulders in their own right and most, if not all, are still quite large stories. However, we are drilling down into our parent boulder-level story and establishing a nice hierarchy of more detailed understanding.

There are two activities that can help us break these rocks down into pebble-level stories. Having the team estimate them always helps. First, the estimates will clearly tell you whether the rock will fit into your sprint length. If it doesn't, then you are truly forced to break it down further.

Even then, you don't want to fill your sprints with rocks that need the entire sprint to complete. That sort of end-to-end execution dynamic would be a very risky proposition and would potentially defer done-ness and delivery far too late in the sprint. Point being, you want a wide variety of smaller sized stories (executable pebbles) to effectively load-balance and fill each of your sprints.

But, estimation certainly helps drive the discussion and further decomposition. The other activity that helps in decomposition is writing solid acceptance tests for your rock-level stories. Let's do one as an example using this rock-level story:

> *As a writer, I want to allow for various attributes: underline, bolding, sub/super script, italicize, etc. so that I can highlight different levels of interaction with my readers.*

We'll start writing acceptance tests for it.

- *Verify that underline works*
- *Verify that bold toggles for all font / color types*
- *Verify that all combinations of all attributes can be combined*
- *Verify that font size changes do not impact attributes*
- *Verify that paragraph boundaries are not effected by attributes*
- *Verify that attributes continue in pre-text, post-text ; for example, if we bold a numbered list text, the number should be bolded*

Now, imagine this rock-level story with and without the acceptance tests. I see it getting quite a bit larger as we peruse the tests and start considering all of the nuance and complexity of the rocks functionality.

Without them, I would have misunderstood its scope and probably have underestimated its size. I would also have had fewer ideas around how to decompose it further; if that was required.

However, with the acceptance tests defined I can start fully considering the overall size and breadth of the story. They drive done-ness checks as well, which this would be an inherent part of our testing and team focus.

Pebbles

So, what would be good pebble-level stories derived from the above rock? Let's attack some of the attribute characteristics individually and see if that helps:

1. *As the editor, allow for underline attributes, so that users can embellish their text…*
2. *As the editor, allow for bold attributes, so that users…*
3. *As the editor, allow for italics attributes, so that…*
4. *As the editor, allow for sub-script attributes, so that*

Since all of these pebble-level stories are somewhat related, I could ostensibly bundle them into a theme. That would make sense in building them and in demonstrating their behavior. It might also make the testing a bit simpler.

I suspect that I could also bundle the acceptance tests for this theme together—simply to reduce the writing I have to do. I'll copy a few of the above acceptance tests that might apply to the theme or collection:

- *Verify that font size changes do not impact attributes*
- *Verify that paragraph boundaries are not effected by*
- *Verify that attributes continue in pre-text, post-text ; for example, if we bold a numbered list text, the number should be bolded*

These are examples of the bundled or common acceptance tests.

Organic Backlogs

In this chapter, I probably gave you the impression that you should always attack creating stories and populating backlogs in a top-down, bolder-to-pebble direction. And, yes, that's one of the more common directions. However, I want you to understand that stories are amorphous. You might find as you flesh-out the details of a pebble that it becomes a bolder that then needs to be re-estimated, re-prioritized, and the decomposition path begins all over again.

This type of recursive decomposition occurs quite frequently when leveraging user stories for your backlogs. That's why I like to refer to the backlog as being organic in nature. You must revisit it continually and be constantly reviewing, collaborating on, and refining your boulders, rocks, and pebbles concurrently.

The challenge is to ensure that the pebble-level stories about to be worked in the next sprint are well-defined and finely grained. Other than that, simply keep "chipping away" at your backlog stories.

Wrapping Up

One of the largest challenges in adopting agile methods is fully grasping the nuance associated with that "simple list" called a product backlog. It's an organic list that the team needs to revisit time and again; breaking stories down and drilling into their details. Not trying to understand everything, but gaining sufficient understanding to: (1) effectively size and plan a story for a specific sprint, and (2) be able to have certain design and construction ideas so that the story isn't a surprise in execution.

The other factor is that stories often (always) beget more stories. For example, as part of the above story, we might write a story related to writing a tool to change font size and attributes dynamically across the spectrum of supported fonts and attributes. This would allow us to automate the process of testing this particular behavior.

As a result, the Boulder-Rock-Pebble metaphor is intended to remind you of the requisite pattern of continuously breaking your backlogs down. So, start breaking down those boulders…and happy mining!

Thanks for listening!
Bob.

Suggested Terminology

1. **Product Backlog** – a prioritized list of work for the team to complete; aligned with a project or application release goal or goals
2. **Backlog Grooming** – periodic visit of the product backlog; refining stories towards execution and delivery; deciding gaps in knowledge and how to fill them
3. **User Stories** – from the Extreme Programming space; a small use case on a card/post-it note
4. **Themes** – collections of User Stories that make sense to implement together; usually driven by demo or testing considerations
5. Story size language:
   - **Boulders** – Very Large stories; synonymous with **Epic**
   - **Rocks** – Medium to large stories; small Epics or larger stories
   - **Pebbles** – Small stories; ready for execution

11—Mature 'Ownership' Of Agile Product Backlogs Isn't Easy

I've come to the conclusion that saying "The Product Owner <u>owns</u> the Backlog…" is the wrong perspective. They should be identified as the "Keeper" or, the "Guide" or, the "Wrangler" or, the "Congressman" of the backlog, rather than the sole presiding "Owner". What seems to be happening with this practice is that inexperienced Product Owners are taking this guidance far too literally, as well as, becoming too heavy-handed in their structuring of the backlog while not fostering sufficient collaboration within their teams and across their organizations.

I've seen patterns where Product Owners:

- Don't effectively listen to their teams' ideas regarding technical debt items such as refactoring code, introducing more test capabilities, or repairing nagging bugs. This often surfaces in backlogs that contain 100% new features and nothing else.

- Push back too heavily on their teams' ideas surrounding bug repairs. Preferring instead to debate quality improvements instead of simply trusting the team to fix them while holding to their agreed quality goals.

- Have flat out control of the backlog; viewing their role as 100% totalitarian—the sole arbiter of business value and what makes the cut. As a result, generating zero collaboration or discussion within their teams.

- Take the position that they either control backlog items entirely OR, abdicate responsibility for items they don't agree with, understand, or support. So, whoever is the 'sponsor' of something they don't agree with or control, is essentially the default Product Owner for it.

- Consider architectural backlog item definition to be someone else's responsibility and don't try to blend these stories with other feature-based stories. Quite often, they want an entirely separate backlog that contains things they truly don't care about.

While I acknowledge that "wrangling" the backlog across many constituencies and still having overall responsibility for it is a tough job, it doesn't necessarily have to lead to these behaviors. Instead, it can lead to a very powerful, servant leadership-focused role where the Product Owner serves as the ultimate collaborative focal point for what surfaces on the backlog.

A Partnership

For that reason, what should be the effective stance of Product Owners?

First, I think they need to adopt a servant leadership mindset—much has been asked of the software management, leadership and project management roles within agile teams. In the servant leader model, it is clearly not "about you". Instead, <u>you serve</u> a constituent team—trying to <u>meet their needs</u> by working hard to aggregate multiple requirements and perspectives into a meaningful, coherent, and valuable product backlog.

Your work and efforts are all for the team. If the team has issues, listen to them and sort out direction based on their feedback. Often you make your trade-offs transparent across team members so they can understand the pressure you might be under, as well as, the drivers behind your decision-making.

Collaboration is central to the mindset, as is trying to achieve broad consensus and understanding. Product Owners need the maturity to realize that the decisions that will come from their partnering with other team members will be greater, and more powerful, than the ones you can come up with solely by themselves.

Another way of saying it is you trust the power of the team. Let me give you an example:

You have a full plate of functional work requested by your CEO in a small start-up company. There's tremendous pressure on you (and them) to get all of it done as soon as possible. The team, when analyzing one of the stories in this work, realizes that they'll have to clean-up a significant amount of technical debt in order to properly implement the story. The difference is roughly 5 story points for hacking up a minimalist solution vs. 30 story points for a balanced, well-engineered solution. Let's just say that the 25 point difference is roughly an entire sprints worth of work for the team—a very significant difference.

So, what do you do? Trust your team and support the work OR, push the team towards the lower point value and commit to cleaning up the remaining points later? What if the team is adamant that it needs to be cleaned up now…what do you do? What if the team really doesn't care so much about the options, which way do you influence them towards?

In listening to the team…have you given them some 'control' over the nuance of the backlog?

I'm actually not going to provide an 'answer' for the above example. It's truly up to you. Please don't say something like "it depends". Rather, take a stance and make a decision!

Earlier on I was sort of joking with replacement terms when I was trying to replace 'Owner' as the qualifier for the backlog. I think a better term would be 'Guide' in that you're guiding multiple constituents and stakeholders (as well as yourself) in a journey to create high value projects and products— and doing so via 'partnership' instead of dictate or control.

Perhaps in the future I'll start using "Guide and Partner" as a better way of describing the essential behavior of the Scrum Product Owner.

Well-Nuanced Backlog

The other important part of the role is the understanding that you need to 'guide' a well-nuanced and balanced backlog. That your job is to gain a stakeholder, business-focused and technology-focused, alignment around what is the most effective layout of work to meet your business, project, technical, and team objectives. That it's not a your versus their view, but rather a shared backlog with aspects that cross-cut all stakeholder needs.

A heuristic here might help. I like to remind myself that going to 100%, or going to 0%, on any specific area of backlog items is very unhealthy condition. For example, if we don't attack technical debt for 5 sprints, then we've skewed the backlog balance towards something else—probably features, so that investment is <u>out of balance</u>.

I'd much rather define a target for technical debt each sprint so that we're continuously improving our application code. Something small, but important, like *20% technical debt and clean-up stories per sprint* [7] would have a very positive effect.

The list below serves as a balanced-reminder of the sorts of things that should be captured on your product backlogs. It's not intended to be exhaustive. However, it should illustrate that there is more work in your "product universe" than simply working on and delivering features.

Product Backlog Nuance or Balance Points

Feature prioritization –
- Business Needs, Minimal Marketable Features; Minimal Marketable Product
- *SWOT* [8] - from a market facing and team capabilities perspective
- Effective decomposition – drawing the value out of (seeing it) in small chunks

---

[7] For example, at iContact we strove for a 20% mix of backlogs to focus on either code clean-up, refactoring, tooling improvements, or infrastructure improvements on a sprint by sprint basis. Test automation infrastructure was a part of this investment. Was there pressure from the product community to 'compress' this? Yes. But having the guidelines in place helped us create a more balanced and maintainable product in the longer term.

[8] Strengths, Weaknesses, Opportunities, Threats—analysis

Quality prioritization –
- Risk-Based testing coverage
- Functional requirement coverage; UAT
- Non-Functional requirement coverage (security, performance, load, usability, reliability, …ility)

Infrastructure prioritization –
- Base software levels, Ex: PHP version
- API evolution & maintenance
- Integrations maintenance

Technical debt prioritization –
- Impact to the teams' progress on future development work
- Past high priority work that wasn't completed properly
- Establishing a pattern or commitment to "beating down" legacy code debt – cleaning it up

Development workflow –
- Architectural alignment
- Design exploration
- Research & Investigation
- Review & discussion

External dependencies prioritization –
- 3'rd party software and + 3'rd party tooling
- Outsourcing of work
- Working with 'external' systems or teams

Team execution capabilities prioritization –
- Balance of the team: Front-end to Back-end to Test to Business Analysis
- Velocity of the team; throughput of the team
- Legacy systems "baggage"
- Complexity of the overall application; complexity of features

By looking at this list, you realize that there is simply no way a single Product Owner that 'owns' the backlog, can effectively serve as the sole arbiter between all of these levels of backlog contribution and nuance. It's impossible. So, where might they look for assistance and partnership?

Leveraging your Functional Managers

There's been quite a bit written about functional management not having much of a place within the self-directed team model of Scrum and the other agile methods. Often the question comes up—"Do they still have a role within agility?" My answer is an emphatic YES to this question. As a Product Owner, I think one of your greatest partners or allies is the various functional managers surrounding your teams. You probably have a software development manager or two, perhaps a manager of architecture or business analysis and, of course, a manager of testing.

Create a shared responsibility between Product Management and Technical / Functional Management in getting backlogs properly aligned by delegating core backlog areas to them. Ask them to work with Scrum Master(s) and their team(s) to contribute effective stories across technical themes that you're generally uncomfortable with from a skills perspective. Work with them on allocation of skill-sets and setting the appropriate balance (percentages) of focus for critical technical areas within the backlog.

For example, ask the test manager to define and present his/her testing strategy. Then activate that strategy by contributing appropriate stories to your product backlog(s). A big part of the business justification, valuation and impact then comes from the test manager describing this to you, the product team, and the overall stakeholder community.

This same thing should be happening with design refactoring activities, UX work, enterprise architecture, and other efforts that are driven by internal (vs. external) needs. The following story illustrates this partnership in action.

A Partnership Story

I was coaching at a company that had a Software-as-a-Service product focused towards the e-commerce domain. It became glaringly obvious over time that the open source database the product leveraged had scalability issues in their design context. As they grew in data and in customers, there were an ever increasing number of performance issues. They ultimately decided to replace the database with SQLServer, which wasn't going to be easy.

We asked one of the functional managers to serve as a "Technical Product Owner" and to write the database replacement stories, inject them into appropriate backlogs across all of the teams, and work with the product organization in balancing this against ongoing feature evolution.

One particular Product Owner collaborated more with the Technical Product Owner because of the nature of the system architecture and where they were starting the database port. I recall vividly how well a partnership those two crafted. They worked hand-in-hand on the backlog—one on the technical-side, the other on the product-side. Both took a global and shared view to "their backlog" so that they could each speak to every story that was being planned and executed.

Whenever I think of partnerships and shared backlog responsibilities being possible and powerful, I think of those two and smile…

Giving up Control…to Gain Control

Part of any shared relationship or partnership is empowering each other to own important areas of responsibility. As a Product Owner, you'll want to give up 'control' of your backlog in order to gain that partnership and shared responsibility. You might ask, what's in it for me?

Well, you'll get help managing your backlogs, you'll achieve better nuance for balanced work coverage, and you'll be improving your teams' ownership and empowerment for the work. You'll also be creating products that are of high quality and balanced in the way in which your customers' problems are solved. In a word, you'll be gaining control by sharing.

But, in giving up control, remember that you're still the primary "Guide and Partner" for the backlog—that you're ultimately responsible for the balance and overall quality. Yes, perhaps it's a thankless role; however, it's also an incredibly important role where your efforts will be noticed and appreciated—by your teams, by your leadership, and importantly, by your customers!

Wrapping Up

So, what did this have to do with the Agile Project Manager? In a word—everything! In agile contexts, project managers often serve in aspects of the role of Product Owner or, are serving a Product Owner, as they build the backlog. Your skills lend themselves directly to thinking broadly and deeply about product depth and broad work / feature coverage.

Also, your facilitative and collaborative skills are priceless when it comes to working on a shared backlog. I hope I influenced your willingness and desire to share in creating a broader and more nuanced product backlog within your broader team. I guarantee you'll get better <u>results</u>.

Thanks for listening,
Bob.

12—Actively Grooming Your Agile Backlogs For Success

In this chapter I want to share some guidelines around creating sound product backlogs for your agile teams. While this is certainly the realm of Product Managers and/or Product Owners, it also falls to the Business Analyst to assist, or 'own', the backlog details within agile teams.

In general, I find that teams spend too little time grooming. This leads to problems such as:

- Painfully long sprint planning meetings
- Little pre-thought being placed into designs
- Poor planning and execution
- Lack of creativity when solving business problems
- Poor release forecasting

Therefore, if those are the problems, what might be the solution? I, along with many other agile coaches and trainers, use the term grooming to refer to the *activities that surround creating and maintaining* [9] your agile product backlog. I intentionally overload the term; let's explore what I mean by grooming your backlog.

---

[9] Many teams forget the recommendation in _Agile Software Development with Scrum_, the first Scrum book, surrounding backlog management or grooming. In it, Schwaber & Beedle spoke about 10% of the teams' time being dedicated to grooming activities. That's "off the top" of time allocated for each sprint; or 4 hours per team member, per week.

What is Backlog Grooming?

Think of backlog grooming as something beyond a simple requirement definition. I like to think of managing the product backlog as part requirement development, part project planning, part implementation strategy development, part risk planning, and part architectural and design exploration. Perhaps, that's why so many teams new to the agile methods struggle in their sprints—because of too narrow a view to activities surrounding "backlog management".

The easy part for most teams is the requirement part, i.e. writing the user stories. They're quite used to that. However, based on most of the literature on backlog development, these teams are told they're done with the backlog when it's full of prioritized stories. I actually believe that's just the beginning.

So what else should happen in grooming?

Maybe the best way I can explain it is to make a list of the 'happenings' that should be occurring in typical backlog grooming meetings between the Product Owners and their teams. That's where we're going next.

Estimation

A common activity that happens frequently is estimating *user stories* [10] in which the very popular planning poker technique is used. The key to effective estimation is the conversations that occur across team members surrounding each story. It's quite normal, and healthy, for the team to discuss design, acceptance tests, testing requirements, risks, and even who might be the best person to work on the story.

The estimation drives all of these rich discussions, as well as, when to and how to effectively split or decompose stories that are too large. Remember that estimates can happen multiple times on stories whenever the team feels a new sizing would help them in decomposition and more detailed understanding.

---

[10] While I typically use User Stories as the defacto standard for product backlogs, Scrum uses the term PBI or Product Backlog Item to refer to items on the backlog. Point being, they don't have to be user stories, but can be any unique characterization of work for the team to complete.

Decomposition

Related to estimation and the timing for when a particular story may enter the team for development, is the breaking down of epic-level stories into stories sized so that they can be executed and delivered within a sprint. This is one of the more challenging areas for most teams as it requires ongoing practice, and iterative review of the stories, while the team makes progress and gains understanding, as the application unfolds.

Architecture and Design

It's a myth that agile teams figure out architecture "as they go". Teams should identify the cases where they need architectural or, design look-ahead, in their early backlog grooming efforts of epics. In these cases, the team can either initiate a Sprint #0 to clarify larger areas of ambiguity, or explore prototyping and experiment, OR they can create research / spike stories that allow for that sort of thing on a more finely grained basis. The key point is that these sorts of discussions are healthy and necessary as teams actively guide the emergence of their systems and component designs.

Readiness Criteria

A notion that I see more teams using today is sprint readiness criteria for sprint execution. Yes, having clearly defined done-ness criteria is important, but perhaps even more important, is determining whether a story is crisply defined enough to be effectively worked in a sprint. Defining a set of readiness criteria helps determine if a story is adequately refined. Many teams feel pressure to enter stories prematurely and then pay the penalty with excessive misunderstanding-driven rework. The sad truth is that these stories "were not ready" for execution and should have been held from the sprint.

Just to help make this point, here's an example of user <u>story readiness criteria</u>:

- The story is well-written; and has a minimum of 5 Acceptance Tests defined
- The story has been sized to fit the teams velocity & sprint length: 1-13 points
- The team has vetted the story in several grooming sessions—it's scope & nature is well understood

- If required, the story had a research-spike to explore (and refine) it's architecture and design implications
- The team understands how to approach the testing of the stories' functional and non-functional aspects
- Any dependencies to other stories and/or teams have been "connected" so that the story is synchronized and deliverable
- The story aligns with the Sprints' Goal and is demonstrable

Unless every story passes this checklist, it will not be allowed to enter a teams' next sprint.

Risk Planning

I've never really liked the notion of traditional risk planning where you make a list of potential risks, determine plans for what you might do if they occur, and then waited for each risk to trigger or occur. Agile risk planning is much more intentional and proactive than that.

As part of grooming, the team should be placing stories in sequence so that they're actively discussing and reducing overall risk. They should be front-loading complex or ambiguous stories so that they're done early in the release cycle. Or, splitting stories into research-spike stories where they clearly don't have a clue on how to approach building the story. Risk potential and mitigation becomes part of the conversation for each story, sprint, and release the team plans together.

Improving Team Skill-Sets

I often get asked how agile teams should handle the situation where each person on the team is a 'specialist' in an area of the application—a front-end UI developer, versus a back-end developer, or database engineer. In these teams, each individual has typically defined themselves by their functional skill and knowledge within the domain and application. The complaint usually is that everyone can't work together because of these skill-set specializations or boundaries.

My response is usually the same. It's a team's responsibility to work as a team to solve their customers' problems. Therefore, a part of backlog grooming should consider opportunities for cross-training and cross-application knowledge transfer—so the team becomes more nimble and can get more done via swarming on the work. Then these opportunities for skill improvement are exploited when the team plans each sprint.

Sprint Game-Planning

An extension to discussing skills as they relate to the work coming into the team, is game-planning the next sprint. I usually take some time in the grooming meeting, right before a sprint, to allow the team to discuss their strategy for tackling the sprint as a body of work. Often, efficiency is a part of the discussion—meaning I want the team to think about optimizing their throughput and workflow. So, pairing and collaboration are aspects of that. I also want to hear a little about risk mitigation and developer to tester collaboration. I actually think it's a healthy pattern for the team to enter their sprint planning with a big picture idea of the overall body of work and how they plan to attack it—as a team.

Conveyor Belt Workflow

An analogy that I'm using quite a bit lately for the product backlog is one of a conveyor belt. The belt is continuously moving epic, course-grained stories forward in time for the team to break them down until they enter and are delivered from a sprint. I think stories should be examined several times by the team as they move forward towards the sprint. As you'll see below, I have a health metric that stories should be 'seen' by the team four times between the initial epic definition until they're finally groomed for sprint execution.

During this time, the team is increasing its attention to the stories and working details. Another important part is to map each story back to any business committed release plans. Keeping those more holistic scope commitments in mind and communicating clearly when the scope of a story changes and impacts the overall release plan. A simple way of saying it is that grooming itself is a highly iterative and transparent feedback loop.

I hope all of these ideas influence your thinking about your backlog grooming sessions, as well as, the activity itself. You may not consider all of them, but perhaps you might add one or two of them to your grooming sessions.

In the spirit of this thread, I want to now share some 'smells' to look for that will give you an indication that you're backlogs are "well groomed". The following is a list to keep in the back of your mind while grooming.

What ARE Some of the 'Smells' of Well-Groomed Backlogs?

1. Sprint planning is incredibly crisp, short and easy; usually taking 2 hours or less for a 2-week sprint. There are NO architectural or design discussions within the meeting—the relevant parts of these discussions having occurred earlier.

2. As a daily occurrence, team members are talking about epics and stories targeted for 2-3-4 sprints in the future. As a result, everyone is naturally aligning with the Product Owners' vision.

3. The team easily contributes new stories to the backlog which represents non-feature based work; for example: testing artifacts, non-functional testing work, refactoring, automation development, performance tuning, research spikes, etc. Everyone views it as a shared responsibility.

4. The team has a feel for where the product is going long term and maps efforts, designs, theme suggestions, and trade-offs towards that vision.

5. Each sprint's goal is easily derived from the backlog; i.e., there is a sense of thoughtful and meaningful story collections or themes that easily surface from within the backlog. From time to time, think of these as "packages" for customer delivery.

6. The Product Owner includes team feedback (bugs, refactoring, improvement, testing, etc.) in EVERY sprint—in some percentage of focus. They clearly show the team that they are listening and acting on their feedback, judgment, and technical opinions.

7. The Product Owner rarely changes priority of elements purely because of size estimates. This doesn't include breaking them into "now versus later" bits. Illustrating that priority is mostly driven from external business needs that are translated into stories.

8. Blitz planning is done every 2-3 weeks, not only as a planning tool, but also as a risk or adjustment tool. For XP folks, consider release planning as being a similar exercise. The point is end-to-end planning towards the next release milestone occurs iteratively and frequently.

9. Teams are hitting stretch items and pulling in more work per sprint. There is an enthusiasm to deliver more towards goals by creatively trading off story sub-elements. Of course, all of this is heavily collaborated with the Product Owner.

10. The backlog is mapped to the teams' skills and capabilities, stretching them – yes, but not asking them to do things they are not capable of doing either by skill or experience.

11. Within every sprint, the Product Owner is making micro-adjustments to scope based on interactions with the team. Always striving for that Minimal Marketable Feature and Product set!

12. The team is never surprised in sprint planning. Not even by a single story. I know, change is supposed to happen, but surprising the team with last minute changes…is not! Instead, make it wait till the next sprint.

13. The team feels they have a say in what's on the backlog and the distribution of features vs. improvement items. However, they can't be solely parochial in their views. They need to make a business case from the customers' point of view, for all non-feature work introduced into the backlog; they do this willingly and effectively!

Wrapping Up

For you Agile Project Managers reading this, you might be asking yourself why should I care about the product backlog? That's the domain of the Product Owner. To that response I say…wrong!

The backlog IS the project plan, the risk plan, the workflow and collaboration plan, as well as, the overall strategy for how an agile team will be attacking their work. Yes, of course, it contains requirements (user stories). But, it also represents all the notions I've just mentioned. I believe your job is to partner with the Product Owner and the team to make the backlog representative of all of the above.

You have the skills to do it, and hopefully now you have some of the rationale behind doing so and some ideas as to what a 'good' backlog should really look like. Now, go out there and create truly excellent backlogs!

Thanks for listening,
Bob.

References

I thought it might be useful to share a few references on approaches for splitting up user stories. Here's a sampling that should prove quite useful:

1. http://www.richardlawrence.info/2009/10/28/ patterns- for-splitting- user-stories/
2. http://agilepainrelief.com/notesfromatooluser/ 2010/12/more- notes-on-story-splitting. html
3. http://www.agileforall.com/2009/12/10/new- to-agile- learn-how- to-split-stories/
4. http://lassekoskela .com/thoughts/7/ways-to- split-user- stories/
5. http://xp123. com/articles/ twenty-ways- to-split- stories/
6. http://blogs. collab.net/agile/2012/06/20/15- ways-to-split- an-epic-a-team-exercise/
7. http://blog. gdinwiddie. com/2011/05/01/splitting- user-stories/

Section 4 – Mindset

This is probably one of my favorite sections of the book. It shares specific stories, lessons, and approaches surrounding the mindset of more mature agile teams. Now, I don't want to come off as a perfectionist here, nor as an agile purist, however, there are many extremely competent agile teams around that might not exhibit all of these traits…all of the time.

That's ok. In fact, it's probably the normal state. But, I do think this section is representative of some of the key aspects of the agile mindset.

13. Do You TRUST Your Team?
- http://www.projecttimes.com/robert-galen/the-agile-project-managerdo-you-trust-your-team.html

14. Fail Now as a Strategy
- http://www.projecttimes.com/robert-galen/the-agile-project-managerfail-now-as-a-strategy.html

15. What's the Big Deal about Commitment?
- http://www.projecttimes.com/robert-galen/the-agile-pmwhats-the-big-deal-about-commitment.html

16. Getting Out of Jail Free
- http://www.projecttimes.com/robert-galen/the-agile-project-managergetting-out-of-jail-free.html

Enjoy!

13—Do You TRUST Your Team?

As an agile coach, one of my favorite expressions in response to nearly any situation I encounter within agile teams is—"trust the team" or "trust the process". Here are a few examples of what I mean:

If you think your team has underestimated their work and are leaving velocity on the table, just "trust the team"…

- *If they have underestimated their work, they can always pull in more. Besides, you could also be wrong. Allow them to sort through how they understand, size, and execute their work. They'll appreciate the trust you've given them and will invest in doing the best job they can.*
- *If you do see poor estimation or poor execution and adjustment, then bring this to the attention of the team so they can explore it within their retrospectives. Give them examples, but allow them to explore the most effective way(s) to improve. But, expect them to improve!*

If you feel that the team isn't working hard enough or are committed enough to their work, "trust the team"…

- *Unless you're a direct member of the team, it's fairly presumptuous of you to assume they're sand-bagging and not working hard enough. Or else, thinking that they lack commitment. Instead, observe how hard*

they do work, handle their challenges, and deliver on their sprint commitments. Assume that the wonderful professionals you've hired are just that—hardworking, honest, and professional.
- *In addition, remember that, just because people are putting in hours, that doesn't mean they're doing good work or working hard. It just means you have their butt in their seat...not their brain in the game.*

If you feel that quality is poor and it isn't improving sufficiently or that the team isn't taking product quality seriously, "trust the team"...

- *Ensure that your concerns are visible to the team and that they're looking into root cause within their retrospectives. However, let them tailor their activities to improve deliverables each and every sprint. Explore objective data on their defect and quality deliverable trending with them. Give them clear and complete done-ness criteria. BUT, allow them to discover how to do the best job as a team.*
- *Agile is not a magic formula. It cannot take a bad product and, simply because you're 'agile', remove all technical debt and bugs overnight. Improvement takes serious effort, commitment, and time. No silver bullets allowed!*

If you've got to make a fixed date software delivery, and you wonder if the team is going to get there, "trust the team" and "trust the process"...

- *First of all, solid agile teams make everything transparent. Secondly, they approach delivery in iterative chunks. Put these two together and you'll actually get a heartbeat of how well the team is meeting your projections and goals. If they aren't, then you get the chance to negotiate scope trade-offs with them.*
- *Agile projects can ALWAYS hit fixed date targets with fixed costs and quality goals. Furthermore, they can ALWAYS deliver a set of your highest priority features by a fixed date. The variable in these situations, however, is scope. You must be prepared to pare back scope via dropping low priority features and making micro-adjustments to other features—generally delivering "Must-Haves" over" Nice to Haves".*

If you feel that the Product Owner isn't making good decisions surrounding feature priority, "trust the process"...

- *The Product Owner will get plenty of feedback in the Sprint Reviews as to whether they're focusing the team on the 'right' features, at the 'right' time, within the flow of the project. The key is to get stakeholders regularly attending and to encourage continuous and constructive feedback.*
- *Quite often the Product Owner is a surrogate without real decision-making authority. That is NOT setting them up for success. Ensure that your PO's are empowered to make decisions and have the seasoning and domain experience—to make the 'right' decisions.*

These are only a few of the many real-world situations where we have a choice in how we actively demonstrate our understanding of agile principles and exhibit trust to our teams. You see, it's not about <u>saying</u> you trust the team; it's about truly trusting them and <u>demonstrating</u> that in in your words, as well as, your actions.

Next, I want to explore a few, how shall I say it, trust anti-patterns or excuses that I commonly see.

There's Trust, and Then There's <u>TRUST</u>

Here are a few anti-patterns I frequently hear that indicate to me that the organization, leadership, project, management and other stakeholders don't fully trust their teams. I'm sharing them with you to broaden your thinking around trust and the ways we can frame it organizationally. By no means is this an exhaustive list, but more so a list that illustrates how our words don't always necessarily align with truly trusting.

Trust, but Verify...
Of course I trust you, but I'm just verifying that what you're telling me is true—simply as a checkpoint. Don't worry about it, I'm just verifying...

Don't be fooled, this anti-pattern isn't about verification. It's about distrust and the use of micro-management techniques to get into the heads of the team. It's also about control and in what manner they're attacking the project. Yes, verification is important, but not daily. The sprint review is the ultimate verifier. Attend them if you need to see and verify what your teams are finishing.

The process is making me do it …
Of course I trust you! However, I need to get this information into the CMMI Level 3 artifact repository so that we pass our audits. Did you know that an audit was coming next month? Very serious stuff…

Another common anti-pattern is blaming distrust on the methods or process patterns that you've adopted as an organization. We're CMMi Level 4, so I must have you fill out a detailed test results plan and sign at the bottom to confirm that you've tested everything you've said you've tested.

Sure, processes carry some weight and responsibility. But, this anti-pattern extends that as an excuse to hover over the team, and to control approaches and outcomes. Don't allow your processes to be leveraged in this way. Usually there is much more flexibility in fulfilling process constraints than you imagine.

I've been doing this a long time and I know this path will lead to a disaster…
Of course I trust you, but in my 25 years of experience, I've never seen a team deliver on a large scale refactoring effort. I simply don't think it can be done…

While your experience is certainly valuable, times have changed and contexts are different now. Your team is exploring their own experience and finding their way. They need to do this largely on their own…as you probably did.

I'm paid to prevent us from making mistakes…
Of course I trust you, but my job is to prevent us from making mistakes and to develop the best products possible. It's actually in my job description that I lead the team by the sheer force of my will and experience.

Simply being responsible and accountable doesn't give you the right to control all outcomes. In fact, I believe you want your teams to try new and novel approaches. To occasionally make mistakes and learn from them— which lead to much higher performance.

While I honor your job and the description, allowing your teams some "wiggle room" to sort things out on their own will pay big dividends in morale and motivation. Think about how you grew as a leader and who gave you some room to maneuver…

True Trust

In order to illustrate an example of true trust, I have a favorite story I use for describing effective delegation. It goes like this:

> *Delegating is easy when you know how someone will approach the problem you're delegating. Or, when they've been asked to do the task many times before? There is little to no outcome risk.*
>
> *But, what if they would approach the solution differently than you? What if they might try a novel, but risky approach? Or, what if you've seen them fail at this sort of problem many times before? You 'get' the idea…but, you still delegate to them. To me, this delegation, regardless of outcome risk, or approach, is true and pure delegation.*
>
> *It means you trust the individual enough to encourage them to try something new. You're enabling their creativity and will be there if they ask for your help and/or advice. But, they 'own' the task you've delegated to them and, ultimately, the results.*
>
> *Now THAT'S delegation!*

Adapt this definition and re-focus it towards trust. Then, accordingly, start trusting your teams even further. For example, here are a few transitional trust adjustments you might want to make:

- Trust that your teams are estimating work based on the best information they have—and that the estimates are accurate given their context.

- Trust that when your teams run into trouble, they'll let you know and if they need your help. Otherwise, they are making good progress and don't need your 'help'.

- Trust that the transparency of your sprint demos will give you sufficient progress information—both on velocity and quality of the teams' efforts.

- Trust that your teams know best in how to solve product development challenges related to architecture, design, and implementation.

- Trust that your Product Owners are effectively driving customer value and are making the best decisions in balancing business needs against team capacity.

- Trust that your Scrum Masters are emphasizing done-ness, quality, and working collaboratively as a team. That, if something needs attention, they'll raise it as an impediment.

- Trust that when your teams recommend refactoring a component of your system—that it's truly broken and needs attention. Now!

- Trust your teams to trust your own judgment and skills; that they will look to you for high level guidance, goal-setting, support, and impediment resolution. That they'll also look to you for...Leadership and Trust.

A Trust Experiment

One of the attractive aspects of the agile approaches is the notion of short, time-boxed iterations. If you do make a mistake or fail, you can catch it worst case within 2-3 weeks. Only so much can fail. As a project manager, this gives you plenty of wiggle room to allow teams to try things out. To initially trust them, and then to actually see how they perform and react to real results, rather than what you suspect might happen.

Consider this a "safety net" for your agile projects. With it firmly in place, here's the experiment part, why don't you start trusting your teams more?

If they come to you with a whacky idea, or if you think they're not doing what you want, or even something else where every cell in your body wants to interfere...don't! Instead, trust the process and your team! Then, see what happens. The point here is to practice trust to get better at trusting them and the power of iterative development cycles.

Wrapping Up

True trust, like delegation, can be really difficult. As leaders, many of us have engineering backgrounds and are natural problem solvers. Our efforts to engage the team with our 'advice' emerges from our own backgrounds, skills, and interests.

We've also been programmed not to trust our teams. The inherent dynamics of Taylorism and Scientific Management influences our management behaviors when it comes to telling our teams what to do and then, hovering over them until they do it.

However, trust is what a truly empowered and self-directed team needs from us. Of course, you can ask questions, establish vision and set goals, measure results, and provide feedback. You've earned that right with your experience and in your role. Nonetheless, try and give honest trust to your team(s) as often, and as much, as you can. You'll see a huge difference in your teams' performance leading to many positive results. Trust me!

Thanks for listening,
Bob.

14—Fail NOW As A Strategy

Not long ago, I was speaking at a conference and sharing my thoughts on various agile topics. As often happens, a young man stopped me to ask a few questions after one of my presentations. We struck up a nice conversation that eventually slipped out into the hotel corridors.

We started talking about sprint dynamics within Scrum teams and I mentioned that I usually coach teams towards declaring their sprints a success or, pause for meaningful effect, a failure. That we do this as part of the teams' sprint review, with the Product Owner being the final determinant basing it on whether the team achieved their sprint goal(s).

He was quite visibly upset with my view. He said that they (he was working at a well-known Atlanta company) had never failed a sprint. Never! They could not, nor would not, use that <u>word</u> in their culture. I asked him point-blank—"Have you ever failed a sprint?" He said of course they had; many times. But, instead of using the term 'fail', they used the term 'challenged'. That way, stakeholders wouldn't get the wrong idea and question their skills, motives, or the teams' results.

We went round-and-round for another 10-15 minutes in our discussion, but we never really settled our differences. We simply agreed to disagree. Although it wasn't a terribly wide chasm between us, I distinctly remember walking back to my room shaking my head. I simply didn't understand the big deal about failure, about using the word, about a team saying…yes, we failed.

In my coaching practice and in my "day jobs", I've been able to steer and evolve our views so that failure is not a bad word. That is, failure is good. Failure is ok. Failure leads to improvement. Failure is a part of life.

In this chapter, I want to explore failure from a few different perspectives. The discussion isn't intended to be exhaustive. I just want to share my thoughts and to get you thinking about failure; how you view it in your organization, what is your tolerance for it, and re-considering your normal reactions to it. I also think this leads you towards your risk handling as well, because I believe the two are inextricably linked.

Coaching to Avoid Failure

In his blog post from June 20, 2011, entitled _Coaching is Not Letting Your Teams Fail_, Giora Morein makes the case that agile coaches should be leading and guiding their teams away from failure. He brings up the analogy of a Sherpa guiding mountaineers. Yes, in the mountain climbing example, I will have to agree that failure is probably not the result we want.

However, in the non-life threatening cases, I think I disagree with Giora.

I wholeheartedly believe that failure can actually be good for a team. I also think the role of the coach is to help a team look at their performance through two lenses. The easier of the two is the success-lens. This is the lens where you give the team positive feedback and where you tell them that they need to repeat those practices that work for them. Indeed, what practices they need to amplify and do "more of" to achieve greater and greater results while leveraging their strengths.

These conversations are clearly easier.

But what about the failure lens? As a coach, do you provide constructive criticism? Do you show a team where they miss-stepped; both individually and as a team? I imagine so, but certainly not in a malicious or heavy-handed manner. I think if you're effectively coaching a team, you must explore their errors and mistakes, along with their achievements and successes, with equal passion and energy.

Furthermore, I don't think you do this quietly, hiding behind doors and not externally acknowledging their challenges. No. I think you approach it in a completely transparent and matter-of-fact manner. Laying the groundwork that failure is appreciated and welcome. That from it, your teams look for improvement possibilities and move forward quickly towards delivering improved results.

Agile Exposure

In agile teams, there are two key ceremonies that are focused towards success and failure results from a team. In Scrum, that is the Sprint Review (demo) and the Sprint Retrospective (lessons learned). Typically, the sprint review is exposed to the world. Thus, you might want to be careful in how you couch your failures so that stakeholders don't misconstrue the impact or the effort the team is putting forth. Nonetheless, I believe you should declare sprints either a success or failure as part of the introduction to a team's sprint review.

In Scrum, it's the Product Owner's responsibility to determine this; it's relative to the goal(s) the team committed to at the outset of the sprint. Hopefully, those goals were flexible enough to allow the team to adjust their work focus to creatively attain it.

I think a very poor sprint goal is something around the team delivering a set number of user stories—or, other indicators of by-rote execution. This can lead to potential dysfunction on the part of the team to hit a numeric goal, rather than thinking about the true customer problem they're trying to solve. Better goals revolve around achieving some sort of demonstrated behavior (a theme) that solves a specific customer problem.

Success is then measured against how well the team met the spirit of the goal and how well they applied agile principles in their execution. For example, I've seen teams that commit to and delivered ten user stories, but who had an extra three days at the end of their sprint of idle time, fail their sprint. Sure, they delivered to their commitment, but their commitment was flawed. They sandbagged and over-estimated. They also didn't make their additional capacity available to their Product Owner and ask for more work within their sprint time-box. Instead, they planned ahead and/or gold-plated their deliverables.

I've also seen teams that committed to ten stories, but only delivered seven, have a very successful sprint. In it, they worked hard against complexity and adversity. They were incredibly transparent and engage their PO in making daily adjustments on priority vs. their new understanding of capacity. Then, as a team, while they didn't deliver the originally perceived quantity, what they did deliver aligned with their goal and met the spirit of the Product Owner's intent.

Both of these examples should be discussed in the teams' retrospective along with exploring ways to improve. Not in small ways and not ignoring the first teams' behavioral problems. No. All of it—the good, the bad (mistakes and failures), and significant improvement ideas should be examined in order for the team to decide what points are worthy of their improvement focus in the very next sprint.

But, is Failure Embraced?

Continuing with my earlier coaching example, I remember not that long ago I was talking to a group of our Scrum Masters during my "day job" at iContact. If you don't know much about Scrum, the Scrum Master is the primary coach, guide and agile leadership voice within the agile Scrum team. They're also responsible for maintaining core agile values within the team and for the teams' overall performance. What I mean by that is— guiding the teams improved performance over time. Continually asking questions like: is their team improving in their overall performance? Is their velocity improving? Is their work quality improving? Is their teamwork and collaboration improving? Also, is their focus on delivered customer value improving?

My point to the Scrum Masters was that I felt we hadn't failed in quite some time. We had delivered over 100 successful sprints across 10+ teams without a failure. I defined failure in this case as a sprint failure or, a stop-the-line incident, where a team basically ran into an impediment and needed to re-plan or re-align their sprint.

They all agreed with me that things had been going smoothly. I received more than a few questioning stares as to why that was a problem. I tried to be careful in my reply, but my concern was that we might be playing it too safe. That we were becoming too complacent in our agile practices and that we weren't stretching ourselves enough. We weren't taking any chances and, we weren't taking any risks.

I explained that these traits are fundamental to the growth and advancement of agile teams. The fact that we weren't seeing failures was a potential indicator to me that we've plateaued in our growth and performance improvement. I felt this was a problem…and I asked if they could drive more failures from the teams.

Can you imagine the remainder of this discussion?

Here I was the Director of R&D at a successful company talking to my team of Scrum Masters and asking them to drive more failure—to influence their teams towards more risk-taking and inspire more stretch goals. The point I'm trying to make is that I truly embrace failure. That I've learned to view it as a critical success criterion and, that its absence is a problem for me. I wonder how many organizations and leaders have the same view. I even wonder if this is too extreme a view.

The Notion of "Failing Forward"

One of my favorite authors is John C. Maxwell who is relatively well known as a leadership coach and a prolific author having written more than 50 books on various leadership topics. He has a strong Christian background in his life and in his writing. He has also mastered the art of leadership.

A few years ago he published a book entitled *Failing Forward—Turning Mistakes into Stepping Stones to Success*. In it, he emphasizes failure as a truly transformative factor in our personal, professional, and team-based lives. However, he carefully frames failure with a leaning forward posture. That is, instead of viewing failure as a negative end-state and feeling sorry for ourselves, we should embrace it as a positive learning experience. That you should be "leaning forward" in your failure—leveraging the lessons learned to improve.

I don't think Maxwell is simply blowing positive smoke in our direction here. History is clearly littered with examples of successes that were inspired, forged, and hardened in the fire of failure. Thomas Edison is a famous example as he persevered to invent the light bulb.

In my agile coaching I consistently use the terminology "fail forward" when I discuss team-based failures. Yes, I want teams to be honest with themselves and acknowledge that they've failed. But, I also want them to embrace their mistakes instead of getting defensive, blaming others, or denying it entirely. I also want their posture to be leaning forward, to be eager to try something new that will drive different results, and to not be afraid of failure.

I find that using this terminology helps teams to 'get' the nature of failure and to behave appropriately. But beyond terminology, your project and functional leadership need to fully support the idea too—meaning the entire leadership team needs to be supportive of failure. There…I said it.

Wrapping Up

All of that being said, I wonder if I've got a strange and largely minority view towards failure? I wonder if the right response is to indeed be fearful of it, to deny its existence, to spend countless hours trying to predict it, or to never mention it in public. Are those and similar actions the right responses?

To that end, I'm closing this chapter with a request of all readers. I've put together a small, focused survey that I'd like you to take. I know, I know, you're busy. But, I really think your insights will be helpful here. The survey is focused on gathering a view towards organizational, group or team, and individual acceptance of failure and risk. I'm trying to get to a root understanding of acceptance and also the root cause for those views. While I'm particularly interested in agile teams, don't let your lack of agile experience prevent you from responding.

Here's a link to the form -
https://docs.google.com/spreadsheet/viewform?formkey=dDJjeVFST0dDSjJrT0ly M2FmV0IwSlE6MQ#gid=0

What I'll do is collect survey responses, consolidate them, and share them in a future blog post. I wonder if the survey will be a failure.

Thanks for listening,
Bob.

References

1. Giora Morein blog post - http://www.bigvisible.com/2011/06/not-letting-teams-fail/
2. John C. Maxwell - http://en.wikipedia.org/wiki/John_C._Maxwell
3. http://www.amazon.com/Failing-Forward-Turning-Mistakes-Stepping/dp/0785288570/ref=sr_1_1?ie=UTF8&qid=1310263078&sr=8-1

15—What's The Big Deal About Commitment?

As I discussed in the last chapter, I'm a bit of an "odd bird" when it comes to certain aspects of coaching agile teams. For example, I like the notion of calling sprints either a success or a failure based on how the team swarmed around and delivered on their sprint goal(s). Many agilists struggle with using the word '<u>failure</u>' to connote team performance and delivery—some prefer avoiding it entirely.

Another term that causes angst within agile circles is the word '<u>commitment</u>'. Again, I personally like the word commitment. After finishing sprint planning, I like to ask a team to "commit" to their sprint goal. I like the visualization of going "hands-in" as a team—formalizing their commitment. Sometimes teams even physically put their hands together, which always makes me smile.

I see commitment as being a bond within the team to deliver on a realistic goal that they determine as part of sprint planning. It's a bond extended to the business and generates meaning and focus for the team. But again, I may just be odd and miss the true nature of commitment.

What Does it Mean to be Committed?

Let's start with a definition of the term. From wordreference.com I found the following definition:

1. The state or quality of being committed to a cause, policy, or person.
   a. ■ a pledge or undertaking
2. An engagement or obligation that restricts freedom of action.

Given that definition, project leadership is always looking for a team to commit to a project; to its target date or schedule, scope, and cost. They're looking for guarantees from the team to meet the projects' initial views towards completion targets.

On the surface that doesn't sound bad—does it? Bringing it back to software development methods, there's a perceived difference in how "committed" teams are in Waterfall variants vs. Agile variants (Scrum, Extreme Programming, Lean, Kanban, etc.) that I want to explore next.

Waterfall (is) Committed

The thought goes that since Waterfall teams plan their execution thoroughly, to a set of documented requirements, that when the project begins they're in a clear position to fully commit to the project.

They're committed to the date, the scope, and the costs they've estimated. Then, if there is any "negative discovery" along the way, the team will somehow figure out how to "suck it up", work harder and longer to meet their "commitment", no matter what happens along the way!

You'll often hear management driving this behavior—reminding the team of their commitment and to work smarter, but not harder. There might even be veiled, and not so veiled, threats as to what might happen if they fail to— "meet their commitments".

Agile (is not) Committed

Conversely, there's a feeling that agile teams lack commitment. You hear this comment coming from nearly every executive, technology leader, and project manager, who are adopting agile and struggling with forecasting project outcomes.

This comes from the basic tenet that teams agile commit to projects incrementally—as they gain more understanding of the work by implementing it in small chunks. Those teams narrow in on their delivery target as they gain more understanding and collaborate with their customer. Those teams can commit when they've made sufficient progress and understand their delivery velocity.

In lieu of simply committing without knowing, agile teams focus on incremental delivery and incremental commitment; needing some time to truly understand the project complexity and their own capacity. Many misconstrue this prudence and transparency for a lack of commitment. But, there's also a truth to agilists struggling with the term.

A Quick Diversion to the Scrum Guide

Ken Schwaber and Scrum.org have published a definitive reference for Scrum called the *Scrum Guide*. In 2011, they issued an update to the Scrum Guide changing the language used to reflect the team posture at the conclusion of sprint planning. Previous language had used "commit", as in the team would "commit" to the work they identified and planned as part of their sprint.

The updated language changed the word 'commit' to the word 'forecast'. Here's a copy of the language change that I copied from the FAQ on the Scrum.org site:

> *Development Teams do not commit to completing the work planned during a Sprint Planning Meeting. The Development Team creates a forecast of work it believes will be done, but that forecast will change as more becomes known throughout the Sprint.*

This was one of six changes or adjustments that were made within the guide. I bring it up because it amplifies a common negative reaction in the agile community to the word commitment. At my core, I don't understand the issue. It's just a word.

I also think the new Scrum Guide wording sends the wrong message to the team and to leadership in agile environments. I don't agree with the softening of the terminology.

Back to Waterfall vs. Agile Commitment

So, are waterfall teams more committed than their agile counterparts? In the use of language around project targets and scope, it certainly appears so. But, let's get real. Waterfall projects rarely meet their commitments. I rarely do this, but I'll bring out some statistics to make the point…

According to the 2009 Chaos Report examining the success rate of IT projects found that – 32% of projects succeeded, 44% were challenged or failed to meet some project goals, and 24% failed completely.

The key point here is the assumption that these were committed teams, yet literally 2/3 of the projects failed in some capacity. I contend that commitment is simply a word. Now, let's look at commitment from a different angle—probably the _right_ angle.

The Real Nature of Commitment

I don't think team commitment comes from a methodology or a planning process—particularly for highly complex, technology-driven projects, with tremendous up-side risk because your teams are creating novel solutions to customer problems.

Commitment is created by many factors. It seems to me that some aspects of the following are crucial to support an _environment of commitment_:

- Teams _commit_ to work that they have planned and estimated themselves; factoring in their true capacity, and not influenced by unrealistic or artificial targets, from their managers or corporate leaders.

- Teams _commit_ to a compelling leadership vision, which leads to understanding project goals, determines strategies, and, ultimately, measures success.

- Teams _commit_ to each other and, therefore foster an environment of teamwork, mutual accountability, trust, and professionalism.

- Teams _commit_ to exciting and meaningful work; leadership communicates the 'why' and 'impact' of their work to inspire them.

- Teams <u>commit</u> to solid leaders—leaders who trust them to do their jobs and who provide sufficient support for them to succeed. Leaders who are "in the game" with their teams.

- Teams <u>commit</u> to doing good work. Work that balances competitive delivery against solid designs, creativity, work-life balance, and high quality.

- Teams <u>commit</u> to providing total honesty and real-time transparency so that their leaders can make congruent adjustments; to leaders that demonstrate they can "handle the truth".

Wrapping Up

I still like to instill in agile teams that sprints can either "pass or fail" depending on their efforts, behaviors, and results relative to their sprint goal. Furthermore, I <u>do</u> expect a team to "Commit To" their plan to meet a sprint goal that they've established with their Product Owner.

I feel it's not the words: pass, fail, or commit that are the problem.

Instead, the question is—does the environment support the team in the areas mentioned above in meeting their commitments? Point being; I don't see commitment as a team only condition. I think the organization needs to establish a culture and an environment where commitment is supported. Where discovery and adjustment is supported, where honesty and transparency is honored, and where failure is embraced.

If you have an environment that isn't supportive, then yes, I can see changing the term and not using it. In that environment, then "forecast" would be a better term…as would dysfunctional.

However, I'm tremendously disappointed in the organization that can't make congruent commitments across their teams and then deliver on those commitments.

So call me committed to **An Environment of Commitment**…

Thanks for listening,
Bob

References

1. Top 10 Agile Phobias - http://www.slideshare.net/visuri/agile-phobias
2. Chaos Report reference – http://www.few.vu.nl/~x/chaos/chaos.pdf or http://www.projectsmart.co.uk/the-curious-case-of-the-chaos-report-2009.html
3. Scrum Guide reference – http://www.scrum.org/storage/Scrum%20Update%202011.pdf
4. Wonderful article on Estimation, Prediction, and Commitment – http://tynerblain.com/blog/2011/08/09/agile-estimation/

16—Getting Out Of Jail Free

A few weeks ago, I taught a class that focused on agile basics, user story writing, backlogs, sprint planning, and all of the basic operations to kick-off a set of Scrum teams. Everything was going quite well on the first day as I was fielding the myriad of questions that typically come your way.

Then, I got hit with a question that I struggled to effectively communicate a succinct and direct answer to. The question was simple on the surface:

If within a sprint the team can't seem to get the work they planned done, don't you simply put it back on the backlog for execution in the next sprint?

I muddled around for a bit trying to answer the question. I merged my answer with the notion of sprint failure and success. I also spoke about team commitment. Both are topics I've recently covered in previous chapters.

I could tell the questioner was frustrated with my answer—that they simply wanted me to say… yes. Yes, just slide it onto the backlog; that certainly would have been the easier way out for me.

Consequently, we moved on without my providing a clear, definitive answer. But, I've been thinking about this ever since and thought it would be helpful to answer the question in this chapter. Or, at least, discuss more of the nuance behind my broad and feeble attempt at an answer.

Let's First Examine your Commitment

The first part of my struggle surrounds the teams' commitment of delivery towards the sprint goal. Please reference Chapter 13 for much more background here.

The essence is that the team committed to delivering a body of work supporting their sprint goal and I wanted them to do well and to deliver on their promise! I don't want it to be easy for a team to defer work out of their sprints. I don't want them to regularly whine about missed estimates or technical complexity. I don't want them to get accustomed to breaking their promises. I want them to seriously plan, seriously commit, and then, seriously deliver on their sprint goals. Period!

If they do encounter "unexpected turbulence", then I want them to think very hard about how they might be able to adjust to the newfound work and to also think creatively to leverage the ideas of every team member. If they find they need to make in-the-sprint adjustments; then pull the Product Owner into the conversations. As they explore options and alternatives, they should put their commitment and the sprint goal front and center.

Turbulence, I Mean Discovery Happens...Often!

And we need to remember that "s**t" happens within Scrum sprints...all of the time! The teams often find that they:

- Underestimated the work
- Overestimated the work
- Didn't account for technical complexity
- Didn't truly understand the customers problem
- Didn't account for someone taking vacation
- Or, getting sick
- Didn't fully understand the stories
- Didn't groom properly
- Don't have the requisite skills or knowledge to do the work
- Didn't account for testing complexity
- Didn't capture the right acceptance tests

and certainly this list isn't exhaustive. Things come up every day within sprints, which is why I don't want deferring work to be the automatic or default reaction. This sort of "Get out of Jail Free" card isn't the intent of agile nor, does it align with the commitment they've made to their Product Owner and themselves to deliver on the sprint goal.

Now can they move work to the backlog? Sure, absolutely, you bet! Although determining whether or not they should actually take that road, is an entirely different question.

Another Assumption

Another implication of the question is that, if something should slip out of the sprint that it would simply and easily go to the top of the backlog for execution within the next sprint. But that's not always true. Once something re-enters the backlog, the Product Owner has the responsibility to reprioritize it. However, it's their decision as to how to handle the ordering; it may not be as simple as…reprioritize to #1.

For stories that are focused on features to be delivered, the PO may have made commitments to external customers that are difficult to break or re-frame. The other factor is that there may be embedded time constraints as part of the story; meaning, it needs to be delivered by a specific date, or at the end of a specific sprint.

What about the teams' quality values? Should done-ness criteria be easily violated in these cases? Here's an example to illustrate a point surrounding done-ness.

An Example

A team has done-ness criteria established for story delivery. It states that a story will be delivered with no known bugs; i.e., they'll be fixed prior to story completion and acceptance.

Accordingly, the team is working on a two-week sprint. The #2 priority story is predicted to take nearly the entire sprint to complete in sprint planning. The good news is that the team was right on with this one. It's day #8 and the story is nearly complete. The code is complete and multiple rounds of testing have been done. The team is feeling really good about the story and demonstrates it to their Product Owner for acceptance.

The bad news is that there are thirteen known bugs related to the story. They've fixed four of them, but they can't complete the other nine by the end of the sprint. Even more telling, they also uncovered a refactoring effort that needs to be completed as part of re-designing the codebase to support the story. So, they essentially hacked the story into existence and are recommending a fifteen point refactoring story to "do it right" in the very next sprint.

The team feels they completed the story and due to "extenuating circumstances" on day #8 they let everyone know that nine bugs and fifteen points of refactoring needed to be completed before this story is ultimately finished.

I have a few questions for you:

> *If you're the Product Owner, how do you prioritize this new/additional work? How do you balance it against your pre-existing release plans?*

> *From the teams' perspective, did they really finish the story? If not, what should have occurred within the sprint to potentially deliver a more complete story—pun intended?*

> *How would you react or feel if I said the team should have 'swarmed' around getting this story completed within the sprint—no matter what?*

> *And finally, should this sprint be considered a success or a failure?*

The answers are left as an exercise to you the reader. I hope they foster some situational thinking.

Micro Adjustments and the Product Owner

The above example leads into a related idea. I've been using the term "micro-adjustments" a lot lately to illustrate the dynamic between the PO and the team during sprint execution. The notion is that the sprint goal serves as a measuring stick that the team can use continuously throughout the sprint to guide their minor scope adjustments and trade-offs. Believe me—adjustments are certainly required. Actually, not required, they're a fundamental part of the lean nature of Scrum.

So, instead of adjusting whole stories in or out of a sprint, I think the healthier view is for the team to engage the Product Owner as early as possible and/or as discoveries are made within each sprint. For each potential adjustment, the PO and team should examine the issue through the lens of holding the sprint goal intact. Therefore, every trade-off is *relative to the goal*.

If the team can hold the goal by reducing the scope of a feature, then so be it. Next, it's up to the Product Owner to determine if that scope trade-off needs to result in an additional story to the backlog or not. I don't want there to always be a story produced. In many cases, micro-adjustments will result in "good enough" software being delivered at the end of the sprint, with the resulting trade-offs never needing to enter the backlog. In fact, they were never needed in the first place.

The other nuance I was trying to address in fumbling my answer was the notion of micro-adjustments and not falling into the trap of looking at stories as fixed in scope. Instead, the entire sprint is an emergent exercise that is guided by the sprint goal.

My overall experience in sprints is that very little needs to exit the sprint and re-enter the backlog. Sure, there is the occasional bug or refactoring story. Then, yes, stories do occasionally "pop out" onto the backlog. But, the vast majority of the time, the scope trade-offs are internalized and adjustments made that don't ultimately impact the backlog.

Indeed, more often is the case where the team *pulls work from the backlog* [11] into the sprint after they've discovered more capacity versus the scope they'd planned on delivering. Now that's agile!

---

[11] In my own coaching experience of more mature agile teams, it's much more often the case that teams pull additional work into the sprint. Most try to talk about the pessimistic case, as did my questioner, but my experience is that 50-80% of the time teams are stretching more scope into their sprints—so exceeding their sprint goals and over-delivering to their commitments.

Wrapping Up

So, what is the answer? To use my standard consulting answer with tongue firmly in cheek—it depends.

In fact, there are no universal answers to the question. Sometimes it's a perfectly healthy and balanced response to push work from within a sprint to the product backlog. It makes sense and the overall agile integrity of the team is not compromised.

However, in many other cases, this get out of jail free card can have bad side-effects. It puts the sprints success in jeopardy. It can undermine the teams' commitment to results. It can also place the Product Owner in a precarious position. Likewise, it may imply that the team isn't operating with a full "agile mindset" within their sprints.

I would always rather that the team viewed "punting work" outside of the sprint as a last resort—one that was carefully considered and leveraged infrequently.

Now, if I only had a second chance to answer that student's question…

Thanks for listening,
Bob.

Section 5 – Leadership

Lately, I've been reflecting quite a bit on my coaching and what direction it typically takes. In typical agile transformations, II spend about 20-30% time coaching towards the teams and 70-80% of my time coaching leadership (middle management and senior / C-level leadership). Here are a set of topics that I hope will provide guidance towards evolving you into a thoughtful, servant-based, agile leader.

17. How Do You Want Your Software, Good or Fast?
- Choices, choices, choices—We are a product of the choices we make and the constraints we place on a system. So, how do you want your software? Hopefully good and fast; but mostly, good!
- http://www.rgalen.com/blog/2012/6/2/the-agile-project-manager-how-do-you-want-your-software-good.html

18. The 'Essence' of Agile Metrics
- Many organizations struggle with changing their traditional metrics towards more agile-centric metrics. This helps "boil down" the areas that are interesting in agile.
- http://www.rgalen.com/blog/2012/6/2/the-agile-project-managerthe-essence-of-agile-metrics.html

19. Listen to Your Spider Sense
- Agile adoption can have a "neutralizing effect" on leadership in that they don't know when to 'lead' and when to "be quiet". I will try and help you with that dilemma here.
- http://www.projecttimes.com/robert-galen/the-agile-project-managerlisten-to-your-spider-sense.html

20. The Secret Sauce: Team Appreciation
- Saying "Thank You" is one of the most powerful things a leader can do. What's more, it's a responsibility that **everyone** should have.
  http://www.projecttimes.com/robert-galen/the-agile-project-manager-the-secret-sauce-team-appreciation.html

Enjoy!

17—How Do You Want Your Software...Good or Fast?

Picture this...

You are in a software diner one evening after a long day at work. A tired and disheveled waitress walks up to you to take your order—gum smacking as she goes over the daily specials. Nothing really sounds good to you, but you are extremely hungry and short on time. She summarizes the possibilities for you to help with your decision-making. Honey, she says—

You can get mediocre to terrible food fast or slow food that tastes good but, you can't have both good and fast food.

It seems as though we're always given certain choices with our software delivery challenges similar to what our waitress has presented to us. We have all heard of the "iron triangle" or, triple constraint of project management—defining Scope, Cost, and Time as the three critical dimensions for a project. Typically, Quality is placed within the triangle as a fourth variable—mostly at the mercy of the other three.

What is that old project manager joke? You can hold any two of the dimensions fixed, but not all three of them.

But, isn't that exactly what most traditional projects try to do — hold all three constraints constant? What inevitably varies in these constraints is quality, although rarely in a transparent and decisive way. It's usually compromised slowly and disastrously behind the scenes, one method or component at a time, that isn't thoroughly designed or tested or documented properly. These trade-offs always, and I mean always, come back to haunt the team, project, and organization with unexpected re-work.

Badly Influencing a Scrum Team

Not that long ago, I was attending a sprint planning session for one of my Scrum teams. I was the director of engineering and agile coach for a small internet eCommerce company at the time and I liked to hang out as a 'Chicken' in our various teams planning sessions to see how well we were practicing agile.

In the past, we've had relatively mature Scrum teams, so our sprint planning mostly went by the 'book'. The Product Owner would present each user story to the team. The team would ask a final round of questions, to familiarize themselves with the story, and possibly re-estimate it after additional discussion.

After that, they'd plan the tasks for that story and align it into the workflow for the sprint. Frequently, individuals would sign-up for those tasks and realign them based on dependencies and any required sequencing. This exercise would be repeated for all stories until the teams' capacity was 'full'. They would then commit to the sprint goal and set of stories as a body of work to be completed.

In this session, I noticed that the Product Owner was very subtly influencing the team. Let's call him Max. Max was well respected by his team and had established a natural rapport with them. He was also very personable and well liked. During the session, he would talk about the business need for more content in this specific sprint and how desperate the customers were for more-more-more. Also, how important it was to the health of our business. He would always preface team clarifying questions with a level of concern or fear over how much the team might be over-estimating the work. What I observed in the team response was a surprise to me!

They all bought into it!

Often team members changed their time estimates based on his influence. They would all buy into shortening them and, of course, there was always optimistic discussion surrounding the compromise, such as:

- *Oh, we simply overestimated this story in our grooming session— it appears much easier now…or*
- *Oh, Sally is a domain expert here, she can get it done in about one third the time and with less documentation…or*
- *Oh, there isn't as much testing as you might think. Trust us, we'll simply test it with unit tests and a little regression…or*
- *Oh, we don't need to do any design for it, even though it is the most complex part of the system…or*
- *Oh, we can refactor the ugly code in that component at a later time. Don't worry; it's been there for 5 years, what's another 3 months?*

Unbeknownst to Max, he was influencing the behavior of his team in a very negative way. Instead of them being realistic in their estimates and holding to their quality goals, they were succumbing to the perceived needs of the business. Without threats or shouting or coercion, but simply based on his relationship with the team and their desire to 'please', Max wielded great influence.

I clearly saw how the team was shortening their scope on craftsmanship and quality as part of their assessment and planning for each story. Multiply this by the number of stories that landed in the sprint AND the inevitable pressures to deliver, it created a recipe for low quality, high rework, and low customer satisfaction. But, nobody realized it. They kept thinking they were doing what was in the best interest of the business, while also pleasing Max.

The Quality Focused Product Owner and Project Manager

Now, I posit that this sort of influence and behavior is nearly universal in software teams. In traditional teams it's much more open and direct. Max gave us a good example of how there can more subtle interactions within agile teams.

Whether you're in an agile methodology or not, you have the notion of a Product Owner. Call them a business liaison or stakeholder. Call them a Business Analyst. Call them a Project Manager. Whatever you decide to call them, they are the living embodiment of business need facing your teams. They serve as a messenger of need and teams listen carefully to what they have to say—both in their verbal and non-verbal clues and communications!

I think these liaisons can get too caught up in the strain of business and project delivery and then apply the wrong pressure to their teams. Much as Max did in the above story. They think by equally insisting on cost, scope, and scheduling, they'll deliver what the business wants and needs. But, the quality trade-offs this inevitably creates, undermines the very things they're hoping to create.

Instead, they should be demanding that their team holds quality constant; realizing that their teams already understand the need for speed. They should also be constantly emphasizing scope as the variable target for the efforts; that delivering the most valuable components and features first, with high quality, as their "prime directive".

Previously, we explored an example of how subtle messaging around "fast over good" could ultimately back-fire within teams. Now, let's take a look at alternative messaging with a focus on quality.

Be Careful in your Messaging!

You need to be real with your messaging. Teams can sense when you're not being truthful and won't believe what you are saying.

In this trade-off, you also need to be patient and consistent. Conventional software teams have been trading off quality for so long that they don't necessarily see that they're doing it. Or, if they are just beginning to tenuously focus on quality; just one pressured comment in the wrong direction can quickly derail any gains they have made.

With my team example above, in order to turnaround our focus, I interrupted the sprint planning session to remind the team that their purpose was to deliver as much high quality software as they could within each sprint—working as a tightly coupled, creative, and self-directed team. That quality was the paramount factor in every user story. That we wanted, no demanded, that they finish each story to the point of no remaining rework. To use a common agile expression, so that it was done-done-done!

This coaching reminder changed everything and they adjusted their sprint contents and goals accordingly—pushing off nearly 30% of the stories that they would have previously 'committed' to.

I found myself, from that point forward, consistently reminding my teams of this commitment to quality as inherent to agile project success. I would take the time to explain that quality doesn't necessarily result in work taking longer. Since their DNA was so wrapped in making the wrong trade-offs, after years of pressure, I found that for every ten conversations I had on our Scrum delivery focus, nine focused on quality and one focused on content, delivery, timing or speed. When consistently taking this approach, I found that teams began to internalize the messaging and started working in a much more balanced, quality-centered fashion.

Asking the "Right" Questions

To this day, I think this 9:1 ratio is required for most teams transitioning from traditional to agile methods. Instead of Product Owners, Project Managers, or leadership focusing so strenuously on schedule, cost and/or scope, they should be focusing on QUALITY. Questions about quality should be asked often and repeatedly.

Instead of These Questions:

- Are we on schedule? Are you done yet? Are we done yet? Are they done yet?

- What's your velocity? Can we increase it by 50% this sprint? Why can't you deliver twice as many templates as estimated?

- We're behind schedule, what is everyone doing to make it up? Working this weekend I hope!

- Are we working overtime to recover the schedule? Why can't we make the time up in testing?

- What, you want to do some cleanup of hacked code—what will that do to the schedule? Can't we just wait?

- Is that work on the Product Backlog? If not, we can't do it. Or, another variation…Is that on the Roadmap?

- We are committed to this date and delivering specific content…period! Are you part of the solution or part of the problem?

- We don't have time for architecture or backlog grooming in this sprint…we need to simply "Get 'R done!" Are you with me?

Ask These Questions:

- Have we reserved time to plan for testing? We're going to vet that plan across the team…right?

- Did you vet that feature with the customer? Is it what they were looking for? Oh, they want changes, more than we planned for. Well, don't let that influence our doing it 'right'!

- Did you deliver complete unit tests with the solution? Did they all pass? I'm glad. Now we just need to maintain them in future sprints so we have an effective "safety net".

- Did the team sit down during the design of the component and review / collaborate on it? Did you post those design decisions and notes on the wiki?

- Did you meet your done-ness criteria…before I sign off on this story? Anything you wish you would have done, but didn't?

- Were there any refactoring opportunities as part of this story? What would that cost us in time?

- Did you test it thoroughly? Did you document your tests in some fashion – acceptance tests, test cases, etc.?

- Did we do a code review? Did we make all of the noted adjustments? Did we re-review the code if appropriate?

- Are we moving too quickly or chaotically? Do we need to slow down a bit and re-focus on our quality and craftsmanship?

Do you see the difference? How hard would it be for you to reframe your typical project or team inquiries in this fashion? What impact would it have on <u>your</u> teams?

Remember—Trust and Engage your Testers!

There's a partner that we often forget in our teams. It's the testers! Why do we traditionally discount them so quickly? I think a part of it has to do with the balance that we're discussing here. When you're balancing towards speed, you don't want to hear anything that might potentially slow you down. In addition, testers, whether you know it or not, are all about slowing the train!

They find bugs. They constantly talk about up-front quality and baking it into the project rather than testing it in. They want us to test thoroughly and document the results. They gulp…want to get things right the first time.

So, if you are emphasizing quality within your teams, guess who becomes a wonderful partner in your efforts? Gulp again…your test professionals!

Instead of trying to marginalize or ignore their feedback, which I see far too often, encourage, ask for, and even demand their feedback. Realize that they want to get the project done as quickly as you do. They just want it to be done well. Ask them for strategies to holistically deliver a solid product. Speak to them about historical trends and what risks they perceive will uncover in your current project.

Above all, don't short-shrift their time needs. Give them the time to do a solid job and setup your project culture so that their feedback is listened to and applied.

Wrapping Up

I'm of the mindset today with my agile teams that I can get good software and can get it sufficiently fast and/or fast enough. Teams certainly 'get' the <u>fast</u> part of that equation—especially since our traditional approaches to software have beaten it into their conscious and subconscious so well over time.

The point is—I believe we need to, by default, slow things down just a bit. Yes, I just said that. Although slowing down doesn't necessarily imply non-competitiveness or becoming truly slow. It simply means that we're balancing across good and fast and delivering things that are <u>Good and Fast Enough</u>. Fast enough implies a thoughtful balance between cost, time and schedule and, more importantly, scope – one that accepts ongoing adjustments based on incremental progress towards a clear goal.

We also need to emphasize the commitment that we (the business) have toward <u>good</u> to offset our historical bias toward fast. It's the recognition of our DNA and the power of asking the right questions from key stakeholders that can lead us towards effectively balancing across these four project dimensions. Is that too much to ask?

Having a nice meal and getting it quickly enough? Patty, my waitress, doesn't think so any longer and perhaps neither should you…

Thanks for listening,
Bob.

18—The 'Essence' Of Agile Metrics

I've been struggling for quite some time now figuring out the "essence of" agile metrics. What are good ones versus bad ones? Are there related sets that are relevant and how many are needed? Also, how much change do we need to make from our traditional metrics thinking towards agile and team-centric metrics?

One thing I have discovered is that metrics need to be '<u>different</u>' in an agile organization or culture. Traditional measures don't seem to work within agile teams, as I've often seen them cause dysfunction (more on that later) if unadjusted for agile contexts.

Another thought I've had is whether they should represent a trailing indicator or a leading indicator? Meaning should we measure the processes <u>at the beginning or leading edge</u> or, should we focus more on the results and learning <u>at the end or from the trailing edge</u>?

One seems to be more interesting to me and drives healthier behavior, which we'll explore next.

Leading versus Trailing Indicators

I think of measuring estimate accuracy (estimate + actual) as a leading indicator. Why is that since you measure actuals at the end of your work?

I'm thinking of it from the point of view of what you're trying to improve. In this case, you're measuring estimates and actuals to improve your overall planning and estimation processes. These activities are typically front-loaded actions and are often static; meaning they are completed once at the beginning of the project.

The other challenge with this metric is taking corrective action for improvement. You can effectively only make a change with the next planning interval for your next project. Depending on the length of that interval, improvements could be infrequent and/or delayed. Or, depending on project success, they might not be useful at all.

I've also seen some agile teams that have tried to measure various things. Here's a typical example—

> *How about we measure user story volatility in the sprint?*

What they're trying to focus on, is how many times stories change (get added, become reframed, reduced in scope, or removed, entirely) within any particular sprint. To what end? Well, we'd like to improve our story grooming process and monitor how the team is delivering on their sprint planning commitments.

Ah, there's a key—sprint planning is sort of a leading indicator; in this case, you're measuring the quality of story entry. What if we turn this into a trailing, result-oriented, measurement? Let's measure the velocity of the team as they exit the sprint. We can measure velocity in stories produced and in story points delivered.

An even better trailing metric is to measure how the team delivered value towards their sprint goals. Meaning, did they deliver what they had committed to? Not in tasks or in stories, but in content that exactly met the spirit of their customers' needs, as well as, the level of their commitment. Plus, did they deliver the highest priority (highest value) stories first—with lower risk and greater visibility and collaboration?

You notice that I reframed the notion of a trailing metric to a result-oriented metric. Another way of thinking about it is measuring at the "outbound side" of the team's work. That way, you're leaving the responsibility of the work up to the team and simply measuring results or outcomes.

Let me provide an example of why this might be better. Let's go back to the example I gave above. What's wrong with measuring story volatility?

On the surface it appears fine. We can see how well the Product Owner staged the sprint and also how well the team is interpreting stories for execution. For example, if they "signed up" for ten stories, but only delivered seven because of story (requirement) volatility, then they have a lot of improvement to do…right? Well, that _could be_ the case.

However, it could also be the case that the team trimmed those stories because they were superfluous to the customers' needs. Meaning they were essentially a waste. Or, another positive interpretation of it could be that the team leveraged their creativity and figured out a way to meet the spirit of the sprint goal with fewer stories. In fact, they may have even trimmed out some previous code in order to simply the application and so the overall produced lines-of-code count might be quite low too.

Can you see the point I'm making? I find that leading indicator metrics can sometimes be more prone to metrics dysfunction than trailing, results-oriented metrics.

In his book, Measuring and Managing Performance in Organizations, Robert Austin coined and explored the term metrics dysfunction. In simple terms, it's a metric whose collection influences the very behavior being measured—leading to metrics dysfunction.

One of the classic examples of it is measuring software testers by the number of bugs they find. In this case, testers would report more trivial, non-germane bugs simply to hit the metric…and in the meantime they'd miss truly important bugs. Clearly not what the measurer intended!

In our example, the leading metrics might influence the team towards not changing stories that need to be changed but, simply to hit the metric of stories being consistent with the views from planning. I can see nothing more destructive to the agile mindset of the team than having metrics that drive negative behavior within the team—simply to meet, or game the metrics.

So, what are some potentially **unhealthy leading metrics** to avoid within agile teams?

- **Planning quality** – measuring how well you planned. An important part of this is change control, i.e. measuring how little or much change is ongoing.

- **Requirement quality** – measuring whether each requirements meets some sort of baseline definition or completeness. Or, that each has a specific number of acceptance tests.

- **Estimation quality** – I've emphasized this point in the chapter— effectively anything that tries to measure estimation variance with actual effort.

- **Arbitrary results** – Counting lines of code produced, bugs found, or requirements written—virtually anything that is materially produced by the team where you negate the quality of the result and the application of common sense in that not all results need the same level of attention and thinking.

Conversely, what are some potentially **healthier trailing metrics** to concentrate on within agile teams?

- **Team agitation levels** – capturing multi-tasking events, number of committed hours per sprint and variance from expected levels; for example, unexpected recruiting support for team member or training interruptions.

- **Team velocity levels** – trending over time, improvement trending (implying improved team dynamics), paying attention when team composition changes. Compare velocity trending relative to agitation levels above.

- **Impediment handling** –number's per team, average time to resolve, and number(s) that impacted the Sprint Goals. Discovering whether you are removing the most critical obstacles as aggressively as possible for each team.

- **Retrospective actions** – are the teams improving themselves based on retrospective results, how many improvements per sprint, average time to resolve. Are they seeing the expected results from these adjustments?

- **Escapes per sprint** – bugs found post-sprint, adherence levels to Done-ness Criteria and identifying and correcting reasons for not supporting complete done-ness.

- **Sprint Success / Failure** – from the perspective of the Sprint Goal. Not so much focused at a story or task completeness level, but at an _overall work delivered_ level relative to each team's goal.

One of the things you'll notice with trailing indicator metrics is that there is an inherent real-time nature to them. We want to be sampling them (observing, discussing, driving action) each and every day during each iteration or sprint.

I believe it's this level of team awareness of their performance (metrics) and active engagement towards continuous improvement that is the key to healthy metrics in an agile context.

Agile Metric Categories

Another healthy discussion relates to what type of metrics to collect from an agile team. I've seen many examples that recommend the following areas as places to focus your attention:

- Quality Output
- Team Health
- Value Produced
- Throughput, Capacity, or Predictability

Having these categories in mind when you're establishing what to measure within your agile teams, gives you a broader and healthier base for your observations and thinking.

I normally try to create 1-2 metrics in each category that we pay attention to as an organization. Any more than that and I find we lose our focus and the metrics don't drive the conversations and improvement we need.

To give you a real world example, when I was at iContact for a time, we measured the following in our agile team KPI's (key performance indicators):

- The number of sprint escapes per team, both defect escapes and process escapes—for example: times when the team ignored our Done-Ness Criteria. (*Quality*)

- Story cycle time / Work-in-Process or WIP limit; we created an aggregated metric that accommodated the different sizes of stories and examined well we maintained a healthy WIP within our teams. (*Throughput*)

- Sprint value delivery in stories / features delivered to our release plan. Our Product Owners maintained this metric—reporting on earned value of features relative to our committed release plans. (*Value Produced*)

- Interrupt rates or churn within our teams. While we were a mature agile organization, we sometimes suffered from excessive team member movement from team to team and interrupting team members for "fire-fighting". (*Team Health*)

We didn't care about individual data points or measures. Instead, we were much more interested in trending over time—either sprint by sprint, or across our release tempo. We were looking for gradual but sustained improvement.

If we didn't see that improvement, we didn't penalize or 'fire' anyone. Instead, we simply looked for the root cause and asking why was this trend happening? We were curious and continuously looking for ways to improve.

That, or whether the metric was indeed useful, and/or whether we needed to change it to something better, would drive our improvement insights in other directions. We were ever curious about our metrics and willing to change our focus, and what we measured, as we discovered more about our overall team performance.

Wrapping Up

While applying traditional metrics to agile teams can drive dysfunctional behavior, agile teams still need some sort of measures that guide their improvement. They also need balanced leadership that can protect them from overreacting to short term interpretation. This is where a seasoned Agile Project Manager can really make a huge difference in an agile environment.

In helping the team select a small, core set of critical measures and helping them pay attention to the metrics trending and to inspect, adapt and improve based on what the data is showing them. Consider yourself the dashboard for the team that keeps them on the road, at the speed limit, and ticket free.

Thanks for listening,
Bob.

Here's a wonderful Dilbert that nicely compliments this topic - http://imagininghistory.blogspot.com/2011/07/why-there-is-more-to-organization-of.html

19—Listen To Your "Spider Sense"

A few weeks ago, I was working with an organization on a coaching assignment. They had been experiencing quite a bit of attrition within their technology teams and discussion inevitably went to root causes. Most of their leaders were confused about the drivers behind it.

One of them said that they had sat down with several developers before they resigned and everything seemed fine. They talked about the developers' concerns and tried to address every one. They felt that there were "tuned into" the team and were trusted. They just couldn't understand why people were leaving without giving them an earlier warning, and more importantly, a chance to address their concerns.

There's another interesting 'twist' to the plot.

The company had recently run an employee survey in which the entire technology team seemed happy with their salary levels. They also expressed the general feeling that they were competitively compensated. Therefore, everyone within the general management structure of the company, took that "off the table" as a potential issue.

However and here's the "Spider Sense" part, the technology leadership team at the company knew the following:

- Local hiring for software talent was 'hot' and the company was an attractive target because of the talent of their engineers. The company was viewed as a high-growth startup.
- Several key ex-employees had poached multiple engineers to their new organizations. This had been significantly on the increase over the past year.
- In all cases when departures were made, it was heard through the 'grapevine' that money was a significant factor. Although the staff, while fairly paid, were not paid at a "premium rate" sufficient to compete in the hot local compensation market.

So, as not to belabor it, the teams were telling leadership that compensation was not an issue. Yet, team members were leaving for significant compensation increases. Was compensation an issue?

From a raw, surface level data perspective, the answer was <u>No</u>.

From an astute technical leader reading the landscape, along with their local environment perspective, leveraging their observations, knowledge of their teams, and lastly, using their spider sense and their instincts, the answer was a resounding <u>Yes</u>!

The company will continue to lose people until it does something about their lack of compensation competitiveness; amongst probably other adjustments. It may not be the only challenge they face, but it's certainly one of the "root causes" related to attrition.

Where Was I Going with This?

So, what's the point and how is it relevant to the agile project manager? Many naïve and inexperienced agile project managers react to the surface data that they are exposed to in their projects and teams. There's usually plenty of it going on and it usually keeps their day filled with escalations, follow-ups, actions, and goals. It's often incredibly chaotic and hectic, while 'feeling' as if you're well-supporting your team and project.

There's nothing inherently wrong with this. However, what if the "surface data elements" aren't telling you the whole story or truth? What if there are other undercurrents that you should be paying attention to? What if those undercurrents are the "root cause" of your team and project challenges and success barriers? Or, are they the very things standing between your team's ultimate improvement, execution excellence, and delivery success?

I liken this sensitized listening to project undercurrents as developing your Spider Sense. It requires you to read the landscape, listen to the pulse of your team and project, and ultimately put the pieces together based on your experience and judgment. It requires you to hear the unspoken, see the invisible, and sense danger wherever it lurks.

It requires boldness and courage, because often the data doesn't support your instincts and, therefore, you're going it alone. So, what are some of the things you can do to develop your own spider sense? I'll explore a few areas here, but surely the list isn't intended to be exhaustive.

Listen to What's NOT Being Said

Your team is working incredibly well together. Everyone gets along and is quite nice to one another. During every sprint the team struggles, but within each retrospective nothing crucial comes out for improvement. From the teams' perspective and from the immediate surroundings, nothing strikes anyone as needing adjustment or repair.

Still, you get the sense that folks are unsettled. Team members are often frustrated with one another and there's a general lack of attention to quality or detail across the team. In meetings, only parts of the team engage—usually only 1-2 of the loudest individuals. Everyone else seems to be simply along for the ride. The team also doesn't seem appreciative of one another; never thanking each other for help or their efforts.

In this case, the team probably lacks the trust and courage to confront their own performance issues and hold each other accountable. What's not being said is congruent feedback and passionate debate. As an agile project manager, you'll need to look for ways to improve the teams trust and encourage engagement; perhaps levering your retrospectives as the place to drive for more "crucial conversations".

Lack of Continuous Improvement

Many mature agile teams get into a state where they stop improving. Sure, when they're just beginning or converting to agile they often show significant improvement and results. But over time, they flatten out and simply start mailing in their results.

Don't get me wrong. Often they are still a high performing team that is delivering on their promises. But, they're not improving, nor are they 'stretching' in their sprints or taking risks. Often these teams show very little ongoing quality, execution, throughput, or innovation improvement. But then again, they're not regressing either.

You need to lookout for these types of complacent teams and try to use your spider sense to see what might be the root cause.

Often I see leadership mucking things up in teams; subtly taking away some of their empowerment. Burnout is another frequent cause and, yes, you can burn out within agile teams! Another factor might be the product organization not providing inspiration or aligning the teams work towards business goals. Regardless, your spider sense is tingling and you need to explore further and encourage some adjustments.

Product Organization Dysfunction

Too often organizations expect teams to simply "suck it up" and give it their all for the company to get their paycheck. . Today's brilliant technologist and engineers are rarely motivated solely by the money. They want to work on compelling products that delight their customers. They are attracted to product visionaries that are inclusive of their teams. They want to work on great products and they want to be part of the organizations overall success. In a word, they want to work on things that…matter.

In this case your spider sense should focus on how well your business is providing compelling work to your teams. If they're treating your teams like commodities, then you must challenge this complacency and pull someone in to inspire the team by explaining why what they're doing is important.

One aspect of this sense is looking inside yourself as the measure. Are you excited about your projects, the potential, the meaning, and the impact they will make within your company? Are you excited about the difference they will make to you customers? Do you find yourself jumping out of bed in the morning and impatient to get to work? If your answers to these questions are less than stellar, then use your own feelings as a guide on what needs to be done.

Management Dysfunction or They're not listening…

One of the more insidious patterns that I've seen in teams is that leadership is not effectively listening to the team nor taking action. It is perfectly feasible in my entry example, that team members early on shared their compensation concerns with management. But what did management do with that information? If they didn't respond quickly enough or significantly enough, the teams would feel that 'leadership' wasn't taking their concerns seriously.

You see, it's not just about effective listening. Nor, is it about taking small actions or providing excuses. It's really about taking appropriate action that is fast, timely, well-apportioned, and impactful. This tells your teams that you are truly listening to their concerns and that it's worthwhile for them to take the risk in communicating them.

You'll want to pay attention to how leadership 'listens' to your teams, as well as, across the organization. Do they truly listen? Do they plan actions to address impediments and concerns with the team? Do their actions, by and large, align with the needs of the team and are appropriately significant.

I'm not implying that every team-raised issue needs to be attended to. By and large, your teams need to feel that the organization cares and effectively listens or else they will simply just stop telling you the truth.

Trust your "Gut" and your "Common Sense"

These final two areas are my guiding light when it comes to my spider sense.

I often go with my gut feelings in decision-making. They're based on my experience and pattern matching abilities to team and project dynamics that I've seen before. They often focus what I've been observing and condense it into a singular sense or feeling.

For example, I've made three catastrophic hiring decisions in my career. In all three cases, my 'gut' was telling me no, but my head was caught up in bringing those people aboard to ease my short term burden. In all three cases, I ignored my gut feelings; I've never done that again.

Then, there's common sense.

There's an expression in the southern United States regarding pigs. I'll paraphrase it—if it looks like, sounds like, and smells like a pig...it's probably a pig. Too often we complicate things. We try to gather too much data and create a too complex a landscape. The company I alluded to in my opening was doing that. When they analyzed their attrition, they thought they had between 10-15 factors that were driving it and, that the factors were independent or unrelated.

But, when you peeled through the data and got to an honest root cause, there were only three primary factors that were driving attrition—money, the technical challenge of the work, and the company's product vision. I strongly suspect their common sense and gut feelings aligned with those three areas.

Wrapping Up

As an Agile Project Manager, I want you to start leveraging your instincts, experience and skill in gathering the 'smells' within your teams. Just because they're self-directed, it doesn't mean they don't need your experience and help in guiding them through challenges.

Quite often you're in a unique position to see the forest for the trees and pull things together.

As I alluded to earlier, it will often be risky and take courage. Everyone will be off barking in the direction of obvious challenges, while you're guiding them to look in another direction. But, don't be deterred. As that old "Web Slinger" learned long ago…you need to Trust your Spider Sense!

Thanks for listening,
Bob.

20—The Secret Sauce: Team Appreciation

I was attending a session at the Agile 2011 conference where Jean Tabaka, from Rally Software, was talking about some generic agile coaching tools and techniques. Jean happened to mention a few times that Rally had been internally focused on some organizational change models which focused on strengths, positive recognition, and appreciations.

Emphasizing appreciations, she said that it started with team retrospectives. That Scrum Masters would ask the teams to share their appreciations of each other as a start-up or entry ceremony for each retrospective. But, then it caught on within other organizational meetings. She shared that many of their company-wide, all hands meetings began with appreciations.

That it began to change the tenor of the culture—influencing the collaboration, teamwork, and overall energy and results of the company. I came away thinking that I'd been a bit lax in reinforcing "appreciations" in my coaching; she inspired me to renew my focus.

Before we specifically explore appreciation dynamics, there are three trending and related areas that I want to mention. I believe they help support the theme in this chapter and will help you explore this area more broadly.

Positive Psychology and Flourishing

First up is positive psychology. Martin Seligman is considered the father of Positive Psychology and the focus on flourishing and well-being. Two areas of flourishing are of interest in agile teams, or at least, they're the components I've chosen to share in this post.

First, is a focus on positive emotion. This can be 'fine-tuned' in everyone by writing down three positive things that occurred during each day. You can do this via journaling or some other method of capturing team events. However, it's probably best to do this at the end of the day and to focus your mind towards positive outcomes and successes.

The second area is engagement. This can be 'fine-tuned' by preferentially using a person's highest strengths to perform tasks—tasks they would, more than likely, perform anyway. Here you're leveraging your strengths in your role. The agile methods endeavor to maximize positive emotion and engagement as part of the essence of a self-directed team.

Seligman and others have also emerged the term flourishing to represent the embodiment of positive psychology in one's life.

Strengths-Based 'Movement'

This leads quite nicely into the strengths-based and coaching movements. A popular analysis tool is StrengthsFinder from the Gallop people. It's now at a 2.0 level and assesses and finds your strengths as they align with 34 core areas.

Part of the tool, once you've identified your strengths, is to guide you towards leveraging your strengths in your day-to-day work and personal lives. It's my view that you can change (improve) your weaknesses, but it usually takes a long time. And the impact won't be felt for quite some time. However, if you reinforce, or amplify and leverage your strengths, you'll immediately accelerate your growth and impact within your organization.

The point is—amplifying your strengths is a much better way to improve and engage rather than solely focusing on improving your weaknesses. You'll also be happier and more engaged.

Appreciative Inquiry

Appreciative Inquiry, or AI, is an organizational development technique that I've known about for quite some time. It aligns incredibly well in agile team coaching—as do all of these techniques. The central force in AI is running an "AI Summit" where you focus on what's 'right' about an organization and try to amplify it versus focusing on what's wrong and trying to fix it.

By re-framing your group questions towards strengths, you try to:

- **Discover**: factors that are currently working beautifully in your organization.
- **Dream**: (or envision) what processes and/or approaches that might work well in the future.
- **Design**: plan or prioritize those processes or approaches that would work best.
- **Destiny (or deliver)**: the proposed design the group has envisioned.

Nowhere here this did I use terms like "root cause analysis" or fixing problem(s). This lens here is focused towards amplifying your strengths towards even more innovation and results.

Applying AI to Agile Retrospectives

It's a very common practice in agile teams to perform retrospectives that follows a prescribed format of answering the following questions:

1. What did we do well?
2. What did we do poorly or badly?
3. What would we like to try?

If we were to take an AI approach to retrospectives, we'd drop question #2 entirely. We'd amplify #1 to include individuals, the team, and even the organization. Leading the discussions towards strength amplification—or how do we do even better.

The third question is interesting. Very often I find teams coupling #3 to #2, for example—"We really struggled with estimation in this sprint—so why don't we try this technique?" While on the surface it sounds like we're considering positives or strengths but, we're really not.

I'd like to drop the question entirely and reframe it to something like this—

> *What creative and innovative new ideas or approaches can we try that will amplify our strengths and increase our overall results?*

I know, I know, I can get a little wordy. But, in this case, I think the question of reframing focuses the team towards appreciation, strengths, positive improvement, and innovation. A fairly powerful cocktail if you ask me.

Now, let's get back to the original point…

Back to Appreciation

Now that I've established a bit of a research and study baseline for you to explore, I want to get back to the original thesis of this chapter. The point Jean and Rally Software was emphasizing is a whole-team view towards team-mates appreciating each other. Here are some of the characteristics of their appreciations:

- It was given from one individual to another—directly
- The sender and the receiver made eye contact
- It was specific, so a specific act or incident that you are thanking the other person for, was acknowledged
- It's done openly or in public
- The receiver acknowledges the appreciation directly—with a "you're welcome"
- Plus, you do this until you run out of appreciations amongst the group

Quite often, this is a kick-off or initial ceremony—meaning it's done at the beginning of a retrospective or *another more formal meeting*[12]. It has the wonderful effect of warming everyone up and thinking of positive things the team or organization has done.

---

[12] Another place to honor appreciations is the Sprint Review. In Chapter 8 we discussed the formula for powerful reviews. I do think spending some focused times on thanking team member accomplishments in a more public setting can be powerful—not only for the team, but for the organization.

Snowballing

Another observation is that it snowballs over time. In the beginning, teams are often shy, or reluctant, to recognize each other. Often they are afraid to call out someone's positive behavior…I'm not sure why that's true, but it often is.

As this practice is instantiated into each of the teams in your organizational fabric, it gets easier and easier to recognize each other—to be able to simply say "Thank You" for your efforts in a public and meaningful way.

It also seems to change the culture. People start thinking about each other as teammates and not as merely co-workers. They begin to be more observant and thankful for each other's efforts. The daily stand-ups become a bit more positive, results-oriented, as well as energetic.

I've even seen the case that, when the shyness was wearing off, the team's *ability to ask for help increased too*[13]. No longer are team members "holding onto" work too long before raising their hands for help. They realized that they're 'appreciated' even while struggling—that their teammates "have their back".

---

[13] Connect this back to the discussion in Chapter 5 regarding asking for help. Setting up a culture where there is balance in asking for help, saying thank you, and giving help is a crucial step in achieving the agile promise of high-performance, self-directed teams.

Wrapping Up

I think solid Agile Project Managers, more or less, have a visceral feel for when and where to appreciate their teams. They make it situational and appropriate. They also make it immediate, or time-sensitive, because nothing makes a worse impression than thanking someone for something which happened a year later.

Beyond the personal appreciations though, they influence an "appreciative environment" where their teams are kind, gentle, and thankful to each other; where they leverage strengths whenever possible while influencing the teams work. Also, an environment that is infectious in its positive energy and "can-do" spirit.

I'd encourage everyone reading this to invest time in your personal and team-based "appreciations". I'm positive you'll see a difference!

I appreciate you listening,
Bob.

References

1. Jean Tabaka - http://www.rallydev.com/coaches/jean-tabaka
2. Rally Software, - http://www.rallydev.com/
3. Martin Seligman - http://en.wikipedia.org/wiki/Martin_Seligman
4. http://en.wikipedia.org/wiki/Flourishing
5. Strengths analysis tool StrengthsFinder - http://www.strengthsfinder.com/
6. Appreciative Inquiry - http://en.wikipedia.org/wiki/Appreciative_inquiry

Concluding our Reflections

I would love to get feedback from readers. You can do that in a couple of ways:

- You can send email to <u>bob@rgalen.com,</u>
- You can send me comments via the form on <u>www.rgalen.com,</u>
- Or you can comment on the individual blog posts, either on <u>PM Times</u>, <u>BA Times</u>, or my own blog at <u>www.rgalen.com</u>

I also plan on continuing to post updates to reflections reaction, my own and from readers, in my blog at rgalen.com. I encourage you to look there periodically and to contribute reviews, reactions, stories, virtually anything that continues sharing what you and your teams are learning in your agile journeys.

Point being—Reflections is on ongoing process, so please share yours alongside of mine. Let's learn together!

As I said in the introduction, my sincere hope is that you gain some value from the books' topics. The agile methods have been a godsend to me in approaching software projects. I literally can no longer imagine approaching software in any other way.

That being said, they are more philosophy than methodology, more about quality and value, more about continuous improvement, and more about the people.

To the latter point, enjoy your teams and…
Stay agile my friends!

Bob.

Author Background

Robert 'Bob' Galen is an Agile Methodologist, Practitioner and Coach based in Cary, NC. In this role he helps guide companies and teams in their pragmatic adoption and organizational shift towards Scrum and other Agile methods and practices. He is currently President and Principal Consultant at RGalen Consulting Group, LLC.

Bob regularly speaks at international conferences and professional groups on topics related to software development, project management, software testing and team leadership. He is a Certified Scrum Coach (CSC), Certified Scrum Product Owner (CSPO), and an active member of the Agile Alliance & Scrum Alliance.

- In 2004 he published the book _Software Endgames – Eliminating Defects, Controlling Change and the Countdown to On-Time Delivery_ with Dorset House. The books' focus is how to successfully _finish_ your software projects.

- In 2009 he published the book _Scrum Product Ownership – Balancing Value from the Inside Out_. The book addresses the gap in guidance towards effective agile product management.

Bob may be reached directly at – bob@rgalen.com
or connect with him via – http://www.linkedin.com/in/bobgalen OR @bobgalen

Reflections

Reflections

Reflections